INCOMPETENT

Coming Up Short in a World of Achievement

James M. Flammang

TK Press
(division of Tirekicking Today; est. 1993)
Des Plaines, IL 60018

INCOMPETENT:
Coming Up Short in a World of Achievement

Copyright © 2016 by James M. Flammang

Cover by Matt Schwarz
Photo and design by James M. Flammang

All rights reserved. No part of this book may be used or reproduced in any manner whatsoever without written permission, except in the case of brief quotations embodied in critical articles and reviews.

Print and electronic editions published by TK Press
(a division of Tirekicking Today), Des Plaines, IL 60018

First Printing: October 2016

Library of Congress Control Number: 2014916522

ISBN: 978-0-9911263-2-3

CONTENTS

Acknowledgments. v
Introduction. vii
1. Sports. 1
2. Swimming. 8
3. Skating. 11
4. Outdoor Life. 14
5. Boy Scouting. 18
6. Machines. 21
7. Radio Woes. 26
8. Computers. 30
9. Car Trouble. 34
10. Repair Work. 39
11. Making Things. 42
12. Small Talk. 46
13. Sex and Romance. 52
14. Making Friends. 65
15. Keeping Friends. 76
16. Dancing. 82
17. Singing. 87
18. Music. 89
19. Art and Drawing. 93
20. Games. 96
21. Languages. 100
22. Completing Tasks. 103
23. Being Noticed. 106
24. Making Decisions. 109
25. Cooking. 111
26. Cleaning. 116
27. Business. 119
28. Money. 129
29. Public Speaking. 133
30. Learning and Teaching. 137

31. Telephones and Communication................. 141
32. Driving.. 144
33. Having Fun..................................... 152
34. Writing.. 155
35. Dead Last....................................... 160
36. Incompetence vs. Failure...................... 162
37. So, aren't we all good at *something*?........ 165
38. Conclusion..................................... 168
About the Author.................................. 171

Acknowledgments

This book is dedicated to two people. First, to my long-suffering wife, Marianne, who has often cheerfully coped with the after-effects of my imperfections, demerits, and insecurities for four decades. I'd also like to dedicate these words to a good friend, Al Spence, a Canadian cattle farmer and retired high-school teacher. In stark contrast to myself and every other incompetent, Al has been a master of countless skills – someone willing to try anything, and usually succeed. If only a shred of his many abilities had rubbed off on me, there might have been no reason to write this book at all.

Introduction

Some of us can do practically everything. Even more can do a few things well, and qualify as passable in a number of others. Yet another group of folks are able to do several things adequately – sufficient to provide satisfaction and generate rewards, monetary and otherwise – while falling short on the remainder of life's activities.

Then, there are the rest of us.

When the Creator passed out skills and talents, I and other proven, fully-seasoned incompetents must have been looking the other way. Perhaps we were gazing lazily down toward earth. Or, maybe we'd drifted off to a different cloud at that particular moment.

Nonsense, many helpful friends would insist. Everybody has *some* kind of talent, these competent humans believe, and insist – something they are able to do especially well. Not all of them are big, noticeable talents, they would add. But we all have some skills.

Well, no. Sorry. Some of us simply don't know how to do anything in more than the crudest, most ineffectual way, beyond the most elementary tasks of daily life. No one will ever say of us: "Remember him? He was really good at so-and-so." All they'll be able to say is: "Remember him? No, me neither. All he did was take up space, I guess. You hardly knew he was here at all."

Personally, as a child, teenager, and young adult, I had exactly two skills: spelling and math (or more accurately, arithmetic, based upon a general facility with numbers). Though I couldn't handle long numbers like a couple of geniuses on TV in those days, dubbed "Quiz Kids," I could add and otherwise manipulate numbers in my head that other kids could barely deal with on paper.

While in first grade, I solved arithmetic problems meant for seventh-graders. In high school algebra class, the teacher invariably held back the toughest problem until the end of the period, saving it for me. I'd usually have the answer, too. Want to know all the prime numbers under, say, 500? I could have given you a list, without touching a pencil.

At age 11, I was the best speller at James G. Blaine elementary school. Upon winning the district spelling bee that year, I thought I was the best speller in Chicago. Maybe in the country. Soon afterward I was on TV, participating in the Chicago Daily News Spelling Bee. Rather than win, as expected by everyone who knew me, I came in fourth – beaten by two kids whom I'd trounced in our district contest.

Which word tripped me up? Such a simple one: *regatta*. Yet, I'd never heard it before. Regattas weren't part of daily conversation in my working-class Chicago neighborhood.

That's no excuse, of course. Spelling champs, like victors in most arenas of life, have to be able to deal with the unforeseen: in this case, to sound out words that are unfamiliar. Unfortunately, I failed to discern the correct spelling from the spoken word uttered by the person in charge. So, instead of a set of encyclopedias and a trip to the national contest in Washington D.C., I walked away with a pen and pencil set – the same one given to every participant.

This tense experience seemed to be a portent of things to come, and of competence lost. Eventually, someone invented the pocket calculator, eliminating any need for my numerical skills. Then came computers, enroute to taking over the known world and rendering that figure-friendly skill fully obsolete. Next up: the spell checker. Strike down that spelling talent as no longer required.

By then, my own lack of competence in a host of areas was well established, as we'll see in these chapters.

Comedian Lewis Black may have said it best in one of his acerbic routines. Explaining that like a particular group of Jewish people, he's never been adept with machines – or with mechanical devices and operations of even the simplest nature – he admitted that "it's just by the grace of god I can actually wipe myself."

Well, most of us aren't *quite* that ill-equipped, and many of us cannot claim any sort of stereotypical Jewish inability with machines because we're not of that faith. But we definitely get the message, which also has been delivered expertly over the years by Woody Allen in his nebbish persona.

The point of writing a book on such a negative subject isn't just to outline and bemoan all my own incompetencies, of course. We're more high-minded than that ... aren't we? No, our real, primary goal is to note that there are plenty of us incompetents out there, struggling through each day unnoticed, amid a world of high achievers.

Rather than merely recount all that's gone wrong in my life, then, these chapters are intended to provide a bit of solace to younger, up-and-coming incompetents, who have not yet come to grips with their lack of skills. Or, in some cases, are not yet aware of how inept they are, vainly relying on the old adage that "practice makes perfect."

Sorry, strivers. For typical incompetents, a thousand years of practice and trying hard wouldn't elevate us to the ranks of beginner, much less achiever.

Instead of "incompetent," some of the tales in these pages may sound more like a matter of being inept. Or untalented. Maybe unskilled. Whatever the term, in every endeavor undertaken, we incompetents are the ones still stuck on training wheels, long after our compatriots have graduated to exhibiting – if not flaunting – their growing achievements.

Despite all the ludicrous personal imperfections described in these pages, I've managed to earn an adequate living as an independent writer for more than four decades. Partly by choice, but mainly by necessity. Bypassing conventional employment is a monumental bonus for those of us who never felt comfortable dealing with bosses, co-workers, colleagues, clients, or anyone else out in the workaday world. Managing to avoid the indignities of a "real" job for forty-plus years is what made it possible to survive at all. Incompetents who aren't "team players" and don't work well with others can breathe a huge sigh of relief if they're fortunate enough to find a way to support themselves and their families by some sort of independent endeavor.

Better yet, as part of my work as a journalist covering the car business, I've traveled to, and even lived in, places that had been envisioned only as far-fetched fantasy during my growing-up years. I even achieved a minimal touch of recognition in my profession as an author, historian, and journalist. Yes, if fortune happens to smile and we're persistent in our quest to find alternative routes through life, even the most incompetent among us can find ways to lead satisfying – perhaps exciting and stimulating – lives, despite being well-known for excelling at nothing.

If you're one of us – or think you might be – take heart. You are not alone. Within these pages, you'll see just how bad it could be, if you slipped into the ranks of the full-fledged, all-out incompetent.

Astute readers may notice that the chapters are not laid out in particularly logical order. In fact, they appear rather random. Could that in itself be yet another demonstration of incompetence? Maybe so, but the order that transpired played out according to the way the subjects happened to spring to mind; or perhaps, how important each one seemed at the time it clamored for attention.

No matter. There's no reason this book has to be read in any special sequence. When it comes to incompetence, every form is important to the person who has to go through life dealing with it.

To protect the innocent (and the guilty), several names and descriptive identities have been changed or modified. Otherwise, to the best of my recollection, everything in these pages is true. Memory is an unreliable master, though. If some of the participants in my incompetent life were to be consulted, they would present a different view of what happened in the course of a particular incident. Modern research has discovered that none of us remember anything quite as it happened; rather, what we remember is the most recent *memory* of that event.

Along the way toward the goal of edification, may we permit

Introduction

ourselves just a little bit of whining and bemoaning our fate? It seems only fitting, doesn't it? Unfortunately, we prime incompetents aren't even very good at that.

James M. Flammang
Elk Grove Village, IL

1

Sports

"Butterfingers!" Every athletic incompetent who's participated in a sport that involves a ball has probably heard that shrill allegation. It's expressed loudly, by one's peers on the playing field, after the ball has slipped past the hapless player's grip. Chances are, that cry – or one that's similar in nature and tone – was accompanied by a rude, derogatory epithet or two, just in case the point wasn't fully understood at once.

Before long, those who lacked talent yet were tempted to play baseball or softball, in particular, would feel the subtle sting of discontent from their fellows. First off, they'd be among the last chosen out of the total group, by a team leader. Then, team members would be assigned positions: first base, shortstop, center field.

Players who were known or presumed to be especially inept might even find themselves assigned to what sounded like a new position on the field: Left Out. Hint: "Out" did not stand for outfield. Even if such an ousting didn't occur in reality, you could be sure the other players were thinking in that direction.

Singer Janis Ian described the phenomenon especially cogently in the lyrics to her 1975 ballad, *Seventeen*, recalling the pain of inevitably being one of "those whose names were never called when choosing sides for basketball."

Most people develop their sporting skills in school – sometime during their educational years, if not before. For me, it was the opposite. School is what ruined me for sports. Although I probably wouldn't have become a big fan or a skilled participant anyway, school turned me into a devoted non-sporting person.

Not even swimming or auto racing took my fancy, whether as a spectator or participant. As a result, I've long been one of the few professional auto writers who has no interest whatsoever in motorsports.

As a kid, playing on the early postwar streets of working-class Chicago, I was adequate at games and impromptu sports. Never excellent, or even good; but tolerable. Playing softball in the street, where a parked 1938 Dodge might serve as first base, no one ever cringed or complained when I showed up, as far as I can recall. I might not be their top choice for a hastily-assembled team, but the other kids didn't shun me, either.

As soon as semi-organized teams became the rule at James G. Blaine grammar school, a block away from our apartment, everything changed. Suddenly, the class was split – informally but firmly – into those who performed well, versus those who did not. Since it quickly became clear that I wasn't adept enough to be among the first chosen when picking sides for softball, basketball, or any other "ball" (soccer was seldom seen or played in those days), I was relegated to the ranks of the also-rans. Or, more accurately, never-rans.

Now, as they chose their teams, I and several other athletic incompetents would remain standing there at the end, like left-behind idiots, unwanted by either side and accepted only with great reluctance.

For most boys, pickup games were fun; but for sports incompetents, all games were torture. Whether they were organized or not, played with friends or strangers, the distress and humiliation differed little.

Grammar-school sports were nothing compared to the tortures of gym class in high school. The very idea of going to gym class every day was so abhorrent to me that, during my first two years in high school, I opted for ROTC instead. Yes, the Reserve Officers Training Corps. I, who would later become an anti-war protester during the Vietnam era and, later yet, the Iraq War of 2003. After four semesters of that intense military training, under the supervision of some upper-level students who were obviously born to be officers, I decided that even gym class couldn't be *this* bad.

Some high schools focus on football. Baseball is the big thing at others. At Lane Tech High, basketball was the centerpiece of everything athletic. During every P.E. (physical education) class, half the group would play first, while the other half sat in the spectator seats. (This was a large high school with 4,000 students, so the groups in gym class were quite sizable.)

Those of us who were petrified and/or angered by the thought of playing, knowing we would be humiliated one way or another, quickly devised a way to avoid hitting the court at all. When the whistle blew, the first group made its way to the spectator seats, clearing the path for the second group to play for the remainder of the period. Rather than leap into action like our sporting cohorts, our motley crew of incompetents somehow managed – by employing rigorous, innovative techniques to make ourselves virtually invisible to the coaches – to blend into the mob of returning players.

Moments later, we'd be taking our seats as if we'd just finished a strenuous session out on the court. If called upon, when an excessively observant coach was in charge, we might even exhibit a touch of perspiration, backed by a sigh of physical relief, conveying the image of a game well played, with a well-deserved and rewarding rest to follow.

Teachers and coaches knew this was happening, and warned us repeatedly that such antics would not be tolerated. Their words and pleas were futile. We were simply too good at making that transition from outgoing to incoming. We might be worthless with any kind of ball in our hands, but we ranked as all-stars in the quest for avoidance.

Now and then, one or two of us would be trapped, unable to return to our favored seats for a second phase of relaxation, to prepare for the rest of the academic day that awaited. Horrors! We'd have to get out on the court and look like we were playing intently, while actually making a bold attempt to steer clear of that basketball for the next 15 minutes or so. Should someone pass the ball in our direction, we knew just how to avoid having to try and catch it, without looking like we were shirking our sporting duty.

Not every humiliation in the gymnasium involved a ball.

Gymnastics was part of the physical-education curriculum, including a requirement to jump over a "horse." Also known as a "buck," it was a long, leather-covered cylinder mounted atop a set of iron legs.

That forbidding creature managed to look almost as tall as a live horse while you ran toward it, fearful – if you were a boy – that your genitalia would soon be hitting that stiff leather surface painfully hard. Naturally, we were convinced that we'd land incorrectly, atop the beast rather than past it. Provided you were able to propel yourself high enough to reach its upper surface at all, that is. Anyone who's unfamiliar with the device might wish to rent the 1967 movie *To Sir With Love*, where a student jocularly known as "Fats" is goaded by the hard-driving instructor to leap over the buck, even though everyone knows it's way too tall for his capabilities.

For the high jump and other gymnastic endeavors, P.E. students who happened to be left-handed, myself included, were singled out. Rather than taking our turn approaching the obviously too-tall bar from the right, like everyone else, we had to wait until the rest of the class was finished. Only then were we permitted to assault the apparatus, starting from our spot at the left. Actually, going from the left felt like my leg was twisting into misshapen pretzels, thus impairing my ability to get over the bar at all, the first time, much less when it was placed higher yet.

When I attended college at the University of Illinois, two years of gym class were required (except for military veterans). Running a mile was one of the requirements. At that point, in my early twenties, I could barely *walk* that far – and as a former mail carrier, I was a pretty good walker.

Because I couldn't pass the minimum-requirement test, I had to enroll in "basic" physical education for a semester. That meant heavy-duty exercising, which was never part of my daily routine. The fact that we had to leave the classroom area and come to the gym, undress, put on gym clothes, go through the exhausting routine, then shower and dress in street clothes again, was an ordeal that left me worn out and dispirited. To this day, half a century later, I have nightmares about those gym classes.

One semester, for some unfathomable reason, I enrolled in wrestling class. Maybe that's all that was left. Looking back, I can't imagine volunteering to engage in grunting, sweaty combat with another person. After learning a few basic holds, we had our first personal encounter, and I realized that this other fellow wanted to *hurt* me. Nothing else would suffice, and he wasn't about to be dissuaded from his goal of vanquishing me. Like the character in an old comedy routine called "When football came to the University of Chicago," I would have preferred to say to my opponent: "Can't we discuss this?" Needless to say, I didn't last long as a wrestler.

Tumbling was another class that resulted in humiliation and distress. Whatever the opposite of gracefulness is, that was me when trying to do a handstand, a headstand – even the simplest gymnastic maneuver. The acrobats who perform at *Cirque de Soleil* would have fainted away, had they seen me in action on the mats.

Badminton was my choice for one semester. That should have been an easy one, I figured. But I kept hitting the shuttlecock with the shank of the racket, rather than the strung portion. Not the way to get even a modicum of velocity.

As we shall see in the upcoming chapter on Skating, I almost failed to graduate from college because of gym. In my last semester, I had to ask the P.E. teacher if he was going to fail me, because I needed that lone credit to get my diploma. Fortunately, he either took pity on me for my ineptitude, or simply had a less intensive grading standard than I'd feared; so, I was able to graduate as planned, without further shame.

Athletic activities at school weren't the only ones to yield embarrassment and frustration. Being an avid athlete, my father participated in a number of sports, and did so with expertise. Golf was one of them – one of the few that I tried to learn. I can still remember, all too vividly, standing at a water hole, swinging my club ten, maybe fifteen or more times, before finally giving up. With each swing, I either missed the ball completely; or, if I managed to strike it with an oblique blow, it journeyed weakly toward the creek that served as the obstacle, often as not stopping well short of the bank on the near side. I couldn't even hit the ball well enough for it to *enter* the water, much less land on the opposite bank, with the putting green beyond.

Sports fans rule, in both the adolescent world and the adult realm. To be a non-fan in America – or in most of the world – is asking for trouble and embarrassment. Ambling through life as a non-participant might be tolerable, as long as you're a sufficiently enthusiastic fan. That means paying close attention not only to the games but to the players, the statistics, the cosmic significance of it all. To be neither player nor viewer – to ignore sports entirely – makes you a veritable non-person.

My own incompetence definitely wasn't limited to participatory sports. I had no interest in, and knew nothing about, spectator sports, either. Because I grew up near Wrigley Field, home of the Chicago Cubs, it was assumed that I would be a diehard Cubs fan. At worst, I might gravitate one day to the side of another city's professional athletes. Nobody ever imagined that a Chicagoan could be a fan of no sports team at all.

In 1950s and '60s Chicago, the north and south sides were like two distinct countries with little in common. Rarely did residents of one part of the city venture into the other. North-siders were Cubs fans; south-siders favored the White Sox. Period.

On the job, it was assumed not only that you rooted for the proper team, but that you knew all the statistics. Naturally, too, you would need to be informed of the score of today's game practically up-to-the-second.

In bars – especially working-class taverns, but hoity-toity cocktail lounges too, the talk typically turned quickly to the day's sporting events and the latest scores. Sometimes, little else was spoken about – both by those who'd been ace players back in school days, and by those who never "made the team" in any athletic undertaking.

Often as not in those neighborhood drinking places, the talk went a big step further: to illicit gambling on the professional and collegiate games, as well as on horse races. Bookies (bookmakers) could be found at many of the local taverns, including Mailman

Mike, who – after finishing his postal route – sat at the end of the bar all afternoon at the establishment I frequented most in my drinking days.

We won't bother to get into other athletic endeavors that demonstrated utter lack of prowess. Suffice to say that I was a grave disappointment to my father. Fortunately, my younger brother followed in our father's sport-minded footsteps, taking on the athletic mantle that I'd dropped years before and perhaps making up for some of my failings in that direction.

Before leaving the subject, though, one particular physical activity needs to be mentioned: fighting. Only twice have I ever been in a fistfight. Both times, my opponent was a close friend. On both occasions, I was the instigator. Why? Because in my advanced state of inebriation, I was offended by some minor comment that person had made, and immediately determined that only fisticuffs could settle such a dispute.

Needless to say, each time I lost. Badly. In one case, my left eye was so severely pummeled that the eyeball was filled with blood and the eye remained shut for days. Yet, I elected not to see a doctor. Likely as a result, vision in that eye eventually became impaired, to the point that it was twice as nearsighted as my right eye. This has always made it difficult for the eyes to work together properly, making for troubled vision throughout my later life.

Stupid. And I'm not referring to that aggressive opponent.

At least, I never fell into the trap faced by many men, who have only a minuscule bit of athletic ability, yet come to view themselves as just short of pro level, had circumstances only been different. Or at least, they fancy themselves as advanced amateurs. Because the notion of being a working athlete, or a high-level amateur, never even entered my mind, I was spared the heartache of eventually realizing that lack of skill was saying "absolutely not" to a life based upon sports.

2

Swimming

Even in the diverse neighborhoods of defiantly urban Chicago in the Fifties, just about everyone could swim. Except for me.

Among my friends in early teenage years, many of them swam at lifeguard level. Several, in fact, did lifeguard duty at some point in their teens. Yes, officially they were lifeguards, complete with badges to signify their prowess in the pool.

No less important, they *enjoyed* swimming. Looked forward to it. Not only in pools, but especially down at "the lake." That meant Lincoln Park, along the shore of Lake Michigan, in the northern part of the city.

In addition to a couple of long sandy beaches where swimming was permitted, the Lincoln Park lakefront offered "the rocks." Stretching for several miles, these monoliths made up of giant slabs of stone, positioned side by side and haphazardly mortared together, gave Chicagoans a place to stroll alongside the water. Avid swimmers also got an opportunity to dive and swim in more challenging terrain than the family-centered sandy beaches.

To be precise, I *could* swim, after a fashion. Barely. If absolutely necessary, I could make it across the width of a pool. Small pool. Not too deep, preferably – just in case I might panic halfway through and start to sink to the bottom.

My father, meanwhile, spent most summer evenings in Lincoln Park. There, he could swim contentedly, off those giant slabs of stones. He could dive into the water like a much younger man, swim efficiently and steadily, and even float.

How anyone can float remains an undecipherable mystery to me. My wife can float. I've seen her do it. But my inner mind refuses to believe it's possible. Bodies sink. They don't, they can't, remain at the water's surface by staying motionless. They just can't.

Did I ever join my father in that evening activity, which he undertook after a long, hard day of running a paper-cutting machine at a printing plant? I did not. Never once.

Our familial experience in the water together had begun much earlier and less favorably. At about age 5, I was curled into my father's lap as he floated around the edge of Cedar Lake, tucked within a large, inflated inner tube. (Younger readers may never have seen one: a rubbery donut that held the air pressure within a car tire, in the days before tubeless tires.) A small body of water in northwest Indiana, Cedar Lake was a favorite short-holiday spot for working-class Chicagoans in the 1940s and 1950s.

All of a sudden I was underwater, gasping, unable to breathe. No doubt, I was under for no more than a second or two before my father grabbed me and lifted my little body into the air. But even to a little fellow, it seemed like an eternity.

No, I can't really blame that unexpected incident for my inability to learn to swim later on. Not entirely. Still, I've no doubt that it had a bearing on my mistrust of water.

My early experience at the local YMCA didn't help much, either. I registered for swimming class when I was around eight years old, and determined immediately that I didn't like the idea of entering the water at all – and certainly not where it was too deep to stand up.

Surprisingly, we little guys did our YMCA swimming in the nude – no suits allowed. Something of a holdover from naturist thinking that had developed in the 1930s, swimming without clothes was still viewed as more wholesome and healthful in some curious way. Nobody bothered to think about its impact on children who weren't at all comfortable with their own bodies.

Nudity was the rule at our high-school swimming class as well, and here's where the serious trouble started. Because I was a skinny 12-year-old little twerp when I started at my all-boys high school, while other students were 13, 14, and 15, some of them were already well-developed in the masculinity department. Bad enough to have to let myself be put on display at the pool, but the worst part was the showers we had to take afterward. Perhaps that's why, even today, I'm never quite comfortable taking a shower, anywhere. Of course, having seen Alfred Hitchcock's *Psycho* when it first opened in 1960, including Janet Leigh's infamous shower scene, might also have had a bearing on my discomfort when confronting a shower head.

Whereas most Freshmen in swim class whizzed through that bountifully chlorinated water as if they were born to it, crawl-stroking and side-arming their way from one end to the other, the most I ever managed was a thrashing attempt to cross the pool's width. The very idea of intentionally pushing one's head underwater while swimming went against common sense. Heads are supposed to be out in the open air, I believe firmly. That's where the air is. If they're beneath the water's surface, something is going wrong.

Because of my utter lack of prowess in the water, I failed swimming class, and therefore had to take it a second time. Overall, my high-school grades were among the highest in my class; but definitely not in swimming, and not in gym.

Oddly, considering my fear of water, and my grave discomfort when positioned within it, I've always loved boats. Though I still have some trouble accepting the fact that steel-hulled boats are able to stay afloat, I'm quite at ease aboard ship. This is true whether I'm on a rowboat, a sailboat, a ferry, a riverboat – even a canoe. Some of my most memorable days and nights have been spent on a ship, crossing the English Channel or Irish Sea, traversing the Mediterranean between Barcelona and Mallorca, or cruising the harbor outside Veracruz, on the Gulf coast of Mexico. As long as I don't feel at serious risk of falling off the ship and into the depths of the river, lake or ocean, I'm in heaven.

3

Skating

This particular sport deserves a chapter all its own because it's the one and only physical activity – apart from a brief stab at race walking – in which I ever attained a minimal level of proficiency. Not much, to be sure; but compared to the results of all other sporting attempts, my skating efforts were practically Olympian-level.

Okay, to be accurate, at least I reached novice status in ice skating – one of precious few activities of any sort in which I reached any level other than rank beginner. As in, just began 5 minutes ago.

Growing up in working-class Chicago with its harsh winters, ice skating was a popular pastime. The Chicago Park District permitted skating on frozen-over lagoons, including the big one in Lincoln Park, along the lakefront. At smaller parks all over the city, they would spray water around the baseball diamond or some other patch of ground and wait for it to freeze. Then, each afternoon and evening, the skaters would come, ready to brave the cold and exercise their skills on metal blades.

Actual ice-skating rinks did exist, but the guys in my neighborhood did their skating at the public parks, despite the frigid temperatures and hearty Chicago winter winds.

One reason for my ability in this pastime was that, unlike a lot of people who tried, I had no trouble with my ankles. I was able to stand quite easily on skates, with little of the leaning to one side that characterized novice skaters with weak ankles.

No acrobatic maneuvers or showy presentations for me, of course. No backward runs, either. But as long as I kept gliding forward at a modest pace, I was okay.

Incompetent

That being so, I had no hesitation about registering for ice skating as my final physical education class while attending the University of Illinois. Because I'd failed one gym class and dropped out of two others, I was still taking P.E. through Junior year. So, I was pleased to see that they offered something in which I could participate on an almost adept level, though hardly expecting to excel.

I was mistaken. Leisurely skating along in a straight-ahead direction wasn't good enough for this taskmaster of an instructor. No, we had to do little tricks on ice – even skating backwards. The big test involved ice dancing, which is something I'd not only never tried, but seldom even seen done in a serious way.

As a result, the debacle at skating class slashed away any feeling that I might possess even a trickle of competence. Basically, when our turn came for the final exam, I virtually had to be held up by the cute young woman I was allegedly "dancing" with, traversing the rink in a shaky circle of dread and discomfort.

It was not my finest hour. I was so humiliated by my feeble efforts, and so certain that I would fail the class, that I had to ask the teacher if there was a chance I might pass. I needed that credit to graduate, so a failing mark would have been disastrous. In the end, I somehow passed; but that was my last serious attempt at ice skating.

Note that we're talking here only about *ice* skating. Roller skating was quite another matter. As a youngster, I always felt quite uneasy attempting to roll noisily along the Chicago sidewalks wearing clamp-on skates with solid metal wheels. Later, as a teenager, my capabilities did not improve when I made occasional visits to a roller rink, and stepped foolishly into serious lace-up skates. With a wheel at each corner. Rollerblades did not yet exist; or if they did, no one at the Chicago rinks knew about them.

Whichever type of skate was used, I simply couldn't understand how staying up was possible for anyone, let alone an utter incompetent such as myself.

So yes, I would yearn to be like the guys at the Hub Roller Rink, but not the graceful ones who breezed around the wooden oval on wheels with a hot young lady on their arm. No, my envious thoughts aimed squarely at the nattily-dressed dudes in ducktail haircuts, their fluorescent pink shirts tucked casually into tightly pegged trousers with drop loops. Rather than skating, these urban (if not urbane) studly charmers flaunted their jitterbug dancing skills – and good-looking partners – out in the lobby, on a square patch of wooden flooring, to such rhythmic pop tunes of the day as *Marie*, with lyrics by a young Randy Newman. Whether those lucky fellows ever bothered to hit the rink on skates was unsure, but they didn't need to in order to establish a heavy male presence.

Did I ever get up and off the bench and try to ask one of the girls to dance? Are you nuts? In addition to facing the risk of annihilation by a crew of J.D.s (juvenile delinquents) who would not appreciate anyone moving in on their women, my dancing skills were on a par with everything else in my late-teens/early-twenties life. In a word, nonexistent, as we shall see in Chapter 16.

4

Outdoor Life

Some of us are meant to enjoy and savor the outdoors. Others – yes, mainly urban incompetents – are best advised to spend their lives within closed walls. Stay far away from campfires that won't start, trees that defy climbing, canoes that are ready to tip over at any moment.

In a word, nature isn't for us. We're city folk, and proud of it.

Or at least, we can *cope* with the city, despite all its threats and dangers. Plop us down on any street in Manhattan, in Paris, in Mexico City, and we'll probably feel right at home. Barring language barriers, that is, which can make even the most indefatigable urban dweller come close to tears when the words emanating from pedestrians' mouths are incomprehensible. But that's yet another rung on the Incompetence ladder, which we'll reach soon enough (in Chapter 21, to be exact).

For now, let's concentrate on the wilderness. Not too hard, though, because it's scary out there. Urbanites who can dash across midtown traffic at rush hour, locate a café with the best sandwich bread in town, and deal with the most assertive panhandler, may be utterly lost when the sidewalks end and the tree line begins.

What do we find, out in the wilderness? Trees, lakes, mountains, valleys, scenic vistas. Sure, but also torrents of bugs, hungry beasts, lack of comforts, and nonexistent street signs. Plus voracious snakes, cold ground, and rainstorms that could lead to flooding at any moment.

Possibly, a couple of throwback humans like the toothless fellows encountered by the citified canoeists led by Burt Reynolds in the 1973 film, *Deliverance*. Yes, they were exaggerated. Close to caricatures. Even so, they just might be lurking out there in the wild, right behind the next tree, their rheumy eyes scanning the terrain for unwary visitors to harass and humiliate.

I'm an urban guy. That's it. Born in, grew up in an old working-class Chicago neighborhood. In that pre-gentrification era, I got to know alleys, gangways, subway stops, bus routes, expressway entrances. I could have told you the quickest way to get to the downtown Loop, the name of the street just north of Division, or the identity of the takeout joint that created the absolute best Italian Beef sandwiches.

Forage for food on the trail? Far better to hop in the car and hustle over to a strip of restaurants, where a waitress will be happy to feed me. I don't wish to be potential food for a bevy of bears or moose that could be encountered in what is allegedly the great outdoors: the wild, as its devotees call it with good reason.

My father was pure urban, too, having grown up in the very heart of Chicago during the teens and Twenties. Never was he at ease in the outdoors. On rare occasions when our family drove to a summer cabin in Indiana or the upper peninsula of Michigan, my father immediately headed for the nearest bar. For the duration, he spent most of his time there – just as he did back home.

My mother, in stark contrast, had grown up in the country, in rural Upper Michigan. Her father had been a lumberjack and the non-English-speaking owner of a general store, in a town so small it barely had a name. I never took after her side of the family.

Forests are lovely, yes, in the strictly scenic sense; but creepy, too. Give me an urban alley anytime – even a dark one, in the dead of night, with the inevitable potential for marauders lurking in the shadows.

Long ago, I shared a pup tent at a few campgrounds with a lady friend who loved camping out. After a fitful night in my sleeping bag, I woke up on the hard ground, feeling every pebble and hole. Upon rising, we got to enjoy sharing toilet and wash-up facilities with groups of hardy, outdoorsy folk, each of whom appeared to love the place. Admittedly, the air smelled a tad fresher than what I was used to back in my Chicago neighborhood, not far from the soot-emitting chimneys of active factories. Even so, my idea of "roughing it" was, and is, a black-and-white TV in your motel room, or a set with no cable or satellite connection.

On one occasion during my career as an auto journalist, I turned down an invitation from Kia, the South Korean automaker, to attend a media drive program in South Dakota. Now, that was one of the few states I'd never visited. The car we'd be test-driving was worth the trip, too. Yet, I turned down that invitation. Why? Because I learned that the organizers planned to have us stay in tents. As I heard later, what they called "tents" were sizable and on the luxurious side. Nevertheless, they lacked solid walls; and that was reason enough for me to prefer to stay at home that week.

More recently, I did attend a media drive program in Montana, where we were given a choice: stay in one of their big, well-equipped cottages with all the trappings of comfortable living, or opt for a tent in the great outdoors. Not a pup tent, by any means, but an ultra-luxury version of the canvas enclosure. Glamping, they call it, for "glamour camping."

Despite the promise of comforts within those soft walls, of a decidedly upscale alternative to living rough, to me it was a cringeworthy thought. Therefore, I happily chose the conventional accommodation. Later, I was horrified to learn that "glamping" on that property cost more than staying in a solid structure. For hardened urbanites, there's *never* anything glamorous about camping out, even at a thousand dollars a night.

Part of my job has always consisted of taking four-wheel-drive vehicles through what manufacturers like to call "challenging" off-road courses. There, we make our way through dense woods, along rock-strewn paths, up and down steep mountain grades – wherever the path is gravel, dirt, or nearly nonexistent. Well, l have news for the planners of such events: quite a long time ago, somebody learned to build paved roads, so we wouldn't have to struggle along those narrow, rocky dirt paths in a vehicle of any kind.

Quiet? Pretty? Serene? Could be, but listen closely for the approaching predators of the forest. As for myself, I'd rather hear the groaning squeals of buses and trucks, or even the gunshots of potentially menacing humans. Far better to have to encounter neither one, but the latter rings closer to home.

For the very epitome of outdoor living, of course, nothing beats the Boy Scouts, as we'll see in the next chapter.

5

Boy Scouting

Clearly, I was the world's worst Boy Scout. I claim that award without hesitation, ready to defend my dearth of prowess against any other incompetent former Scout. Therefore, my experience striving for Second Class status warrants a chapter all its own.

In a world where the high-level competents strove enthusiastically to reach Eagle Scout rank, and often did, I barely managed to warrant the aptly-named Tenderfoot stage. Achieving Second Class seemed to be a laughable fantasy. Reaching that plateau meant exhibiting one's talents in the great outdoors, struggling to obtain Merit Badges and a sought-after check-off from the Scoutmaster when (or if) each level had finally been surmounted.

Scoutmasters in charge of Troop 714, which met in a local church basement, were kindly, knowledgeable, and dedicated to their young charges. But some of us were too challenging, even for the best of them.

Mostly, we learned (or attempted to learn) outdoor skills; but Merit badges and stepping stones to the next level covered a variety of areas. Many of them involved cooperative efforts, which was simply not my thing. Already in the early 1950s, we lived in a society based upon social interaction, but I never worked well with others. Still don't, sad to say.

Scout Camp was a particular disaster: both the overnight version where I stayed in bed and missed an exciting hike, and the week-long debacle where I and a boy who lived across the street in our Chicago neighborhood barely managed to find the lake we were supposed to swim in.

(Shades of what would become a lifelong lack of awareness of my surroundings. Just as it's been all my life, I failed to ascertain the layout and the rules right away in Scout camp. Therefore, I felt lost the whole time. Countless more examples would emerge in later life.)

In the course of that initial weekend outing, organizers suddenly announced an impromptu night hike. Everyone else responded with enthusiasm, eager to get out in the woods, craving unforeseen nocturnal adventures. Instead of eagerly joining them, I stayed in my warm, cozy bunk, prepared to sleep the night through.

Not that I was particularly tired, but it was dark out there. Seriously dark. All those creatures that we missed during the day would doubtless be lurking somewhere in that eerie darkness, ready to pounce.

The active group didn't get back until nearly morning, following a long night of adventures, out in the forest. I spent the night cozily comfortable and adventure-free.

Sometimes, those in charge were rather lax and lenient. Or, they wanted even the worst of us to get an award now and then, even if utterly undeserved. That was the case with the Cooking Merit Badge, which I tried for during my week at Camp Kiwanis, out in the boonies south of Chicago. I got validated for my feeble attempt to peel a few vegetables and toss them into a pot of boiling water containing additional edibles. Other, more adept Scouts would soon turn the turbulent brew into a stew to be enjoyed by all. But I got my badge, regardless.

Scout Camp, as mentioned, was supposed to be a week of excitement and adventure. Not for me. A few days into the experience, I placed an emergency phone call to my father, asking him to come pick me up. I was ready to come back to the city, well ahead of schedule.

While at camp, it should be noted, I caught my testicles in a bedspring. (Don't ask!) This sort of incident was typical of my little disasters in life, then and now. Needless to say, I had to go to a medic at camp, struggling to conceal my embarrassment. No great physical harm was done, but considerable humiliation ensued, which took a long time to get over. Maybe I will conquer that

Incompetent

memory one of these days, some sixty years after the incident.

Even today, when older men speak of their childhood as Eagle Scouts, I feel a mixture of admiration and, sadly, resentment. The latter, because those outdoor skills seemed to come so easily to many of the young Scouts.

Before leaving the subject, I feel obligated to point out that there never was even an inkling of evidence of sexual interest on the part of Scoutmasters, or anyone else. This was the late 1940s and early 1950s, when rumors or accusations of misbehavior had not yet come to the public mind – though "jokes" of that nature could inevitably be heard among adolescent boys.

No, all the Scouting leaders (including one of my uncles, who headed a different troop) were simply nice guys, who tried hard to provide an adventurous and memorable experience for their young charges. To them, we incompetent neophyte Scouts had to be a disappointment and an embarrassment.

6

Machines

Even though I had a modest understanding of mechanical matters in grade school and high school – theoretically, at least – making practical use of technology presented some troubling obstacles. Attending a public technical high school in Chicago in the 1950s, every student – even those headed for college – had to take at least four shop classes during the first two years.

(Those whose aspirations after high school were sometimes described in the yearbook simply as "work" slipped into a separate educational program, called "Smith Hughes." They took *mostly* shop courses. Students in college prep classes sometimes joked about the getting-ready-to-work group, declaring them intellectually inferior and unworthy of friendship. That showed how little we knew. In those days, participants in a work-oriented high school program could expect to find a good-paying job immediately after graduation, or even if they dropped out.)

Early inklings of terminal incompetence turned up right away, in wood shop. Each boy had several projects to complete over the course of the semester. Most noteworthy was an allegedly decorative household accessory, which consisted of a trio of wooden letters spelling out the school's initials ("LTH" for "Lane Tech High"). The letters were mounted on a holder consisting of twin wooden strips.

When completed, this creation would be ready for presentation to one's parents, girl friend, or whoever mattered most in your life. Each project had to be hand-crafted from wood, assembled using glue heated in a pot and applied with a brush, sanded and re-sanded ad infinitum to a silken smooth sheen, then varnished carefully to enhance its presumed beauty.

Well, that was the theory. In fact, some of the results qualified as near-masterpieces of the woodworker's art, deftly constructed by young apprentices-in-the-making who had a knack for this sort of thing.

Then, there were those fabricated with a hefty dose of sloppiness, incomplete and inadequate, by the small cluster of incompetents in the class. Our three letters might have been finished – more or less – but chances are, we never got so far as mounting them for presentation and display. Our household accessory had the demeanor of an ambiguous lump that no one could possibly ever want to see, much less display for all to admire. Therefore, we dutifully carried the failed project home, to be tossed into a drawer and never viewed again. At the same time, we accepted a mediocre grade for our efforts, delivered by the ever-critical wood-shop instructor.

Electric shop turned into an even greater disaster. Unlike some in the class, I actually knew something about electricity and electrical devices. I was a Ham radio operator in those days, and had assembled my own radio transmitter, which operated with a telegraph key. I had at least a vague comprehension of how electricity traveled, how radio signals functioned, and so forth.

None of that mattered to my electric shop instructor. All he cared about was how neat our wiring was, when we assembled a device that was laughably simple: a little heater. As it happened, neatness – whether in wiring or other tasks – was not my strong point. In fact, it was my weak spot. As a result, while I earned excellent grades through high school, I barely managed to squeak through electric shop.

Ah, but the worst of all was machine shop. That's where I experienced the true indignity that awaits every incompetent, sooner or later: the humiliation of being pointed out to one's peers as indisputably incapable. Once this occurred, we would bear a mark, invisible but real, that may as well have been the "A" for adultery applied to romantic transgressors in colonial times.

In my case, it was a dual mortification. Here's how it happened. Each boy was assigned to a lathe. Our principal project was making a threaded bolt, of a specified size. Sounded easy enough. And it should have been. Day after day, I toiled with my bolt, running it through the lathe over and over, first to get the chunk of steel down to the correct diameter, then to get the threads just right.

Finally, I was ready. I could now take my bolt up to the instructor for evaluation. This was done not only visually, but by threading a nut of the appropriate size onto the newly-fabricated bolt. "Voila!" he would cry, displaying a hearty thumbs-up. Well, not exactly. This was working-class Chicago, where French-derived words were – well, foreign, and therefore never uttered.

Whatever the word of acceptance was, I never got to hear it. As soon as he attempted to place his nut onto my bolt, we both realized that something was wrong. Not only would the nut not turn, the instructor couldn't even get it to begin. In fact, it didn't fit at all. It couldn't possibly thread onto the bolt, because the bolt was too big!

How could this have happened? I'd always been quite good at numbers, at measuring things. How could I have been so far off in my evaluation of the bolt's most basic dimension: its diameter.

To this day, I don't know the answer to that one. All I know is that I had to slink back to my lathe and effectively start over, trimming the bolt down to the correct diameter this time before attempting to resurrect its reluctant threads.

As if that travesty weren't bad enough, another incident took place later in the semester. After toiling back at my lathe for weeks, trying to redo my bolt (or start over), the instructor appeared to have decided to give me a second chance. "Flammang," he called out one day. "Go to the shaper."

This was big stuff. The machine-shop room was full of lathes. We each had our own. But there was only *one* shaper. This was clearly a huge step upward in expectation, and in prestige.

Even though I wasn't sure I deserved it, in the aftermath of the bolt debacle, I wasn't about to turn down such a highly-prized opportunity. Success at the shaper could even mean establishing a favorable place for myself in the hierarchy of shop class, rather than my current spot at the base of the success ladder.

Incompetent

At first, it went well, too. I got my bar of steel and verbal instructions, and set to work on creating an all-new project. Day One actually saw some progress. If I could just demonstrate my hidden talent on the shaper, maybe my transgressions on the lathe would be forgotten.

Day Two proved to be my Chicago equivalent of Napoleon's Waterloo. When I got to my shaper (I'd already begun to consider it "mine"), I was rarin' to go, eager to whip that chunk of steel into shape. "Let's see now," I wondered. "How do you turn this thing on?" I looked all over for the on-off switch. And looked everywhere once again. In back, down at the floor, attached to the power cord. There was no switch to be found! Time was passing. Soon, the instructor would realize that everyone was busy at their lathes – making sounds of evident progress – while my shaper stood silently idle.

He did. "Back to your lathe, Flammang," he called out, immediately aware of my inability to undertake Step One of the day's work. All because of an elusive on-off switch, my career as a machinist was over before it began. I felt like one of those French Legionnaires in the movies, who misbehaved and had his stripes torn off, right in front of the entire company.

Ever since that day, decades ago, I've had trouble finding on-off switches, whether on computers, appliances, car accessories, anywhere. I swear the companies hide them, just to keep me bamboozled – and unswervingly incompetent.

Oddly, my fourth high-school shop class turned out a lot better, for reasons that remain bewildering all these years later. Only the most optimistic observer could suggest that I gained anything called expertise, yet my finished projects came close to ranking as tolerable. The class was called Aviation Sheetmetal Shop. To my amazement, I suddenly found that I was able to construct the series of projects, using the machines that were required: a drill press, riveter, sander, and more. Why? Nearly sixty years later, I still can't answer that question.

Aviation technology as an occupation was still a relatively new field in the 1950s. Even though the small projects we constructed had little or nothing to do with airplanes, they did permit the development of some basic metalworking skills. None of my demonstrations of those skills turned into disasters, like the bolt that didn't come close to fitting into its mating nut.

No, they didn't look like a journeyman metalworker had made them, but they did suggest the output of a novice; perhaps even a new apprentice. For the first time, I could almost take a bit of pride in what I'd accomplished – a sensation that would not arise all that often in the subsequent years and decades.

7

Radio Woes

Competence with machines and other mechanical skills eluded me outside of school, too – especially when it came to electronic devices. By the time I was in my first year of high school, I'd become an Amateur radio operator – affectionately dubbed Hams in those days. I could send and receive Morse code at a reasonable clip, using a telegraph key of the sort seen in old western movies. I'd passed a written test, and had a neat little license to demonstrate my presumed competence in the field of radio. It didn't take too long to graduate from Novice Class to General Class, either, which included a test of sending and receiving code at a quicker pace: 13 words per minute, if I recall correctly.

Though the short-wave receiver I used was store-bought, I had to install the long wire antenna myself, on the third-story roof of our apartment building. How I managed that task I cannot begin to fathom. Why? Because for virtually all my life, I've been afraid of heights. Terrified. How I could have climbed a ladder to the roof, walked around up there, and affixed the antenna ends to upward protrusions of the building wall – all at age 13 or so – is a mystery. That I got to enjoy being up on the roof, whether work on the antenna was needed or not, defies belief. Maybe my intense acrophobia began later.

Even those who used factory-made receivers were expected to build their own transmitters. Facing that task dredged up memories of my first attempt at building *anything* electronic. It was not a joyful memory.

Each of us has a starting point when it comes to acquiring skills; or in my case, failing in that attempt. My introduction to electronic incompetence came in the preteen years, in the form of a build-it-yourself radio kit, purchased from Allied Radio in Chicago. Following the step-by-step instructions, I dutifully mounted every socket, wired in every capacitor and resistor, attached the tuning unit, installed the built-in speaker, soldered all the connections. Result: what looked like an AM table radio – the sort found in millions of homes in the early 1950s.

Only one problem: it didn't work. After going over every connection yet again, I was at a loss. Each wire appeared to be in the right place, every component mounted correctly. Yet, nothing happened when twisting the on-off switch.

Finally, my only means of resolution seemed to be giving up: to take the inoperative unit back to Allied Radio (the "Radio Shack" of its day), in downtown Chicago, and pay their professional technician to look it over.

So, what was wrong? All my soldered connections, which had appeared adequate to my untrained eyes, were actually lumpy and loose. The tech guy re-soldered every last one, and *voila*! Sound was coming out of that tinny speaker. Yet, now I couldn't consider it to be my own build-it-yourself project. No, logically speaking, it was the technician's. As a result, I chalked this one up as my first big failure and a foretelling of increased incompetence to come.

Could the Ham transmitter work out better? Taking no chances, I picked the most elementary design pictured in the Handbook issued by the American Radio Relay League (ARRL). Even though radio equipment normally used a metal chassis to hold all the components, this transmitter could be built on a wooden foundation, with several rectangles of wood attached together in the simplest way. That looked to be within my meager realm of capability.

Amazingly, it was. It worked. I began contacting fellow Hams all over the U.S. and into Canada, plus an occasional operator elsewhere in the world. I even reworked that first transmitter, moving all the components onto a metal chassis that had previously seen service as a military radio during World War II. Military surplus electronic equipment was a big item in the Fifties, with each component selling for a teeny fraction of its original cost to the government.

Similar success did not come when I attempted to build a more complex transmitter, a couple of years later. Maybe it was all the cheap surplus components I bought for the purpose. If just one of them had been defective, that could have derailed the whole project. Or, who knows, maybe it was my meager soldering skills once again, reviving to halt progress with yet another project.

A few years afterward, I began to lose interest in Ham Radio, though I kept my license active for several decades. At one point, I bought a much-used transceiver (combination transmitter and receiver) at one of the remaining surplus stores, and mounted it in the Chevrolet van that I owned at the time. It looked impressive tucked below the dashboard, with a long whip antenna pointing skyward from the back end of the van. The receiver managed to pull in signals, but the transmitter? That part never sent out a peep, and my incompetence prevented me from making it do so.

Before finally selling the van, I removed the transceiver and antenna – my final attempts at renewing my meager capability in the radio field.

My inability to find the on-off switch on countless machines and devices is only part of the obstacle to comfort with machinery and gadgets of any kind. Locating the coin slot is another. Once, while in Paris for two weeks, I took my clothes to a self-service laundromat. No people were present, but the signs were fairly easy to understand, even with my minuscule grasp of French. With one exception. When it came time to put a coin into the machine, I looked and looked, yet could see no sign of a slot of appropriate size. Finally, I tried to shove my coin into the only space similar to a slot that I could find. So, what happened? It got stuck, halfway in and halfway out, jammed tightly in place.

Only then did I somehow observe the actual coin slot, which wasn't hidden at all. Why did I not see it before? For the same reason that I've been known to crouch and stare at turnstiles in places like the Paris Metro (subway) system, because I couldn't find the slot in which to push my ticket. For whatever reason, such simple receptacles tend to be invisible to me.

As difficult as mechanical and electrical devices have been, they're kid stuff compared to tinkering with computers and modern electronic gadgets, as we'll see in the next chapter.

8

Computers

Yes, I know: incompetence with computers and related gadgets isn't exactly a rarity. For millions of non-techies, especially those of mature years, it's practically a given. Teenagers and pre-teens obviously understand how everything works in this digitized world, but we older folks often are mystified to the point of exasperation.

What makes my computer illiteracy a bit different is that my connection with computers goes back a lot further than most people's. Hard to believe, but I was once a writer of computer hardware and software reviews. Of course, this was back in the mid-1980s, when both of those elements of computer operation were a lot simpler. Though I was never a hard-core techie, I knew enough to be able to write useful reviews for a couple of print publications, as well as develop explanations about how to use various functions.

All of a sudden, not so long after I began, everything started to get considerably harder. Frightfully harder. For software, in particular, I realized that I would have to learn how to use every program before I could write an appraisal of it. Since complexity was rising fast, it was obvious that I wasn't going to last long as a computer-product reviewer. And I didn't, reverting to my previous specialty: writing about automobiles. After all, to write a review of a new vehicle, you don't have to learn how to drive all over again.

Actually, my first experience with computers dates back to 1963, when I was attending the University of Illinois. As a sociology major, I elected to sign up for a class in programming, having heard that computers were expected to be the big thing in the social sciences before long.

In those days, computers were mammoth machines, tucked away behind closed doors. To try out the little programs we wrote, all the coding had to be entered onto punch cards. When your stack of cards was ready, you turned them in at a counter. Hours later, they went through a reader, and your efforts were sent to the Illiac computer down in the bowels of the building. A day or so later, you stopped back at the desk to get a lengthy printout of the result. If you made a single tiny mistake, of course, the whole process had to be done over.

Initially, I couldn't grasp the elemental concept of how a computer program worked. Fortunately, one of my roommates was a math instructor, and a single, cogent explanation by him sent me on my way. Can't say I achieved an overwhelming degree of competence in my study of the Basic and Fortran programming languages (plus another, whose name escapes me). But I got a reasonably good grade, and I still grasp the rudiments. So, score one for a minimal touch of computing competence.

Not that it mattered much, because personal computers wouldn't come into existence for another decade, and didn't start to attract broad attention until well into the Eighties. By then, the languages I'd learned a bit about were mostly dead and gone. Programming was consigned to experts. Early personal-computer users had to learn only a few basic commands to get the machines to perform. Macintosh owners didn't even have to learn *that* much.

As I write this chapter, my two laptops are barely functional, always on the verge of engaging in some form of what can only be considered the computer equivalent of deviant behavior. Odd error messages pop up and won't go away. Often enough, a series of such warnings results in total shutdown, with the risk of losing all that I've been working on. (Fortunately, that seldom happens; evidently, the internal backup systems are at least partially operational.)

With computers, as with most devices, many of us never learn more than is absolutely essential. As a result, we benefit from only a portion of the machine's capabilities.

Most of us don't even know about the additional possibilities that lurk within each device in our possession. They're mentioned and described only within the unfathomable pages of instruction manuals – if there is one. More often these days, the only guides to computer operations are found online, written not by experts who devote their careers to learning and explaining the esoteric details of digital activities, but by amateurs participating in forums. Their words might sound knowledgeable enough, though often filled with typos and poor grammar that make one wonder about their validity. Readers who'd like to know how to undertake a given task with a new program, for instance, can never be sure that the amateur instructor's recommendations will work. They might even make matters worse.

The only alternative is a software or hardware company's support staff, typically reached only by a "chat" session. Or, available at substantial cost. As most of us have learned, their "help" isn't always as helpful as advertised.

Those of us who possess a minimal amount of computer knowledge might find tricky ways to circumvent trouble spots in our computers. It's a lot like nursing an ailing old automobile along, until you're ready to purchase a newer one.

Some years ago, before handheld devices were everywhere, my wife gave me a Palm TX unit. Although I've gotten a lot of helpful use out of it in the intervening years, getting it to function properly was a battle. The kind that makes you want to tear your hair out, if you happen to have enough left to grab.

More recently, purchasing a Nook e-book reader from Barnes & Noble produced a similar result. It works well enough downloading books from the Barnes & Noble online store; and after some trial and error, I found a way to obtain e-books from the public library. But the primary purpose for which I obtained the Nook reader has eluded me, despite a series of unhelpful consultations with support people, store clerks who sell the units, and an e-book expert at the local library. Not to mention tedious use of Google, trying to find advice on dealing with the problem. It's been sitting here for months now, still largely useless.

In stark contrast, the first computer I ever bought – an Epson PC with two floppy drives and no hard drive – was virtually trouble-free. So was my next desktop unit, as well as my first laptops. That was before Windows came in, promising user-friendliness that, for me, just complicated everything.

Yes, I long for the good old days when you had to know a little bit in order to accomplish anything with computers. Why? Mainly, back then, I always knew where my stuff was within the computer's memory. Not anymore. Now, the presence and location of much of it is a mystery. No wonder I still use Windows XP, despite its propensity to misbehave and lock up. I dread the idea of "modernizing," bringing home a new laptop with Windows 7 or 8, which will surely make my worklife even more unfathomable.

Postcript: Soon after writing this chapter, I gave in and bought a Windows 7 laptop. It sat for months, virtually unused, because I couldn't figure out how to transfer my main programs – the ones I use regularly – from my old laptop to the new unit. Finally, I consulted an expert, paying an hourly fee for his advice and assistance in getting the machine running in a useful way – a task that once could have been performed without seeking outside help.

9

Car Trouble

As an automobile enthusiast since childhood, I decided – in the late 1960s and early 1970s – to take some evening classes in auto repair. After a couple of years of class, at two different Chicago technical high schools, I'd say my level of competence reached about 3 on a scale of 10.

Because of my long-standing interest in automobiles, car repairs should have been the one area in which I could demonstrate a bit of skill. Not quite. In my youth, I knew nothing about the workings of gasoline engines, unable to make even the simplest repairs. After learning a bit, I could plod along under the hood, but fell far short of developing anything approaching expertise.

Oh, I could do some basic tasks, such as adjusting ignition points (little devices not used on cars since the 1970s) and replacing spark plugs. Even a brake job wasn't beyond me, provided I had unlimited time for each step. But this was a class that trained prospective auto mechanics as well as do-it-yourselfers. Compared to those in either group, I was like a duffer trying to play golf with near-pros.

Except for the Dodge that I'd damaged at age 15 (see Chapter 32, on Driving), my father had always owned nothing but worn-out old cars. I followed that trend myself, never owning a late-model car until I was a senior citizen. With nearly every automobile I drove, I was the final owner. Next stop: the crusher.

At one point, one of my decrepit old cars "threw a rod" while easing down an Interstate. That's about as serious as breakdowns get, demanding removal of the engine and total dismantling. After arranging with a friend to tow the car, a 1966 Chevelle station wagon, back to Chicago (using a rope), I decided that for a change

I wouldn't call the junkyard to come and pick it up. Instead, because I'd taken quite a few auto mechanics classes by that time, I elected to rebuild the engine myself.

I did, too, with the aid of the very same friend who'd towed the forlorn wagon back to the city. Now, an adept mechanic could have rebuilt the whole engine in a matter of days, if he had enough free time. Well, I had plenty of free time, and it took me a matter of months. Quite a few of them, in fact.

By the time we finished, I didn't even want the car anymore, so I sold it (for a dollar, if memory serves) to that same friend. Though the engine now sounded surprisingly normal, it was burning quite a bit of oil, evidenced by blue smoke out the exhaust every time I pushed on the accelerator pedal. No doubt, my attempts to fit the new piston rings properly had left something to be desired.

Despite its smoky behavior, my friend and his family drove that rebuilt Chevelle to Mexico and back, smoking all the way, and kept it on the road for some time afterward.

That wasn't the only time I wound up giving away a defunct automobile for a dollar, only to see it regain a new life after some major repair work. My 1961 Volkswagen Microbus stopped dead one evening on a Chicago street. This time, a different friend got involved with it and, after I signed the fallen 'bus over to him, he proceeded to rebuild that old air-cooled VW engine (with my help, coincidentally). Took us many weeks, but when everything was reassembled, it ran fine. He and his family drove that Microbus for a couple of years afterward, while I had moved on to my next clunker, continuing my long series of cars that seldom lasted long under my care.

In my teens and twenties, I sent one car after another to the junkyard, even when a minor repair would have made it functional. No wonder I decided to take auto mechanics classes a few years later. Even though I eventually wrote a book on repair of old cars, in the late 1970s – along with dozens of articles on the subject – my own efforts were invariably meager, even after several semesters of busy classes that included plenty of practical work.

Because I favored unusual cars over mainstream models, my

ownership record included a number of foreign-made models, as well as a trio of Studebakers, which were my favorite special-interest automobiles. Preferring cars that were priced below low-budget level, I seldom bought one that didn't "need work," as they were rather euphemistically described in those days.

My 1960 Volvo PV544, for instance, contained an engine that shook severely, causing the long gearshift lever to bang back and forth so violently that I could hardly grab it to change gears. What was wrong? A piston inside the engine had to be replaced, which translated to a major – and costly – overhaul.

A while earlier, my 1957 Renault Dauphine had run only twice during my brief ownership period: just before I bought it, after a long period of watching the previous owner struggle to fire up the engine; and once, after an acquaintance made a few engine adjustments. The Renault also was missing first gear. By that I mean, it couldn't be shifted into first at all, which was no small matter for a three-speed manual transmission.

Unlike most of my cars, which tended to be rusty and tattered, my 1936 Studebaker Dictator looked reasonably good. It should have, because it cost me $1,800 – vastly more than I normally paid for cars.

Viewed more closely, a lot of parts needed replacement, but I didn't care. I loved that car, and simply had to have it. Before I could drive it more than a few miles, however, I had to give it a full brake job, including struggling through a major battle trying to get the brake drums off. Due to non-use, they were corroded in place on the axles. With a lot of help from friends, I did that brake job myself, though it took weeks instead of hours to complete.

Because I began to write professionally about antique and classic automobiles in the 1970s, I became well aware of auto restoration. That means intensive work, demanding substantial skill, to bring an old vehicle back to its original condition, visually and mechanically. Or, more likely, *better* than it was when it first rolled off an assembly line.

Other automotive hobbyists spoke of doing pristine restorations of valuable antiques and classics. I couldn't do the simplest thing, like painting a body panel or repairing a rust hole.

If auto mechanics classes trained me to demonstrate at least a marginal level of competence, trying my hand at auto body work turned into an outright disaster.

One evening in auto-body class, I was allegedly helping a fellow student apply a metal patch over a rustout on his car's floor. He was on his back under the car, holding the carefully-formed patch in place with a tool. I was supposed to heat the patch, so he could apply a brazing rod around the edges, to secure the patch to the surrounding metal.

So, what did my "help" consist of? I managed to burn a hole right through the center of the patch, ruining it.

Because he was a patient fellow, he got back up and set to work making a second patch. Back down on the garage floor again, he got that new patch into position. There I came with my trusty torch blazing, and immediately blasted a hole in that second patch, too. At that point, he decided my assistance might not really be necessary. Who could blame him?

Helping another student with preparing his white Chevrolet for a full repaint, I was assigned to fill a small dent in the fender with plastic filler, then sand the area until the surface was pristinely smooth. Only then could several coats of primer be sprayed on, in preparation for application of new paint to the entire body.

We'd learned that unless the meeting point between filler and body metal was absolutely flawless, the division between the two materials would show through the new paint like a searchlight buried beneath the surface. Guess what? A beautiful paint job, marred only by my utterly incompetent work on that left front fender. I was glad the semester was almost over, so I'd never have to see that student or his car, ever again.

One adept fellow in my arc welding class took to calling me Sparky. He meant well, no doubt; but despite my most ardent efforts, class after class, all I could produce were sparks. No welds. All I can say is, be glad you weren't hanging over the edge of a cliff, clinging to one half of a pair of metal strips that I'd allegedly welded together. You would be in deep trouble, soaring through the air enroute to the base of that canyon.

Naturally, there are many more tales of automotive woe that could be mentioned here. Instead, let's turn to a variety of other incompetence-based disasters.

10

Repair Work

Some people just *know* how to fix things. Even if they've never taken a class, never read a how-to book, never watched a repair being made, they're able to deduce ways to get flawed products functioning again. Often as not, better than ever.

How they acquired such ability and, no less important, the self-confidence to use it, is a dark mystery. Needless to say, I am not a member of that high-competence group of fixers. When it comes to repairs, I am essentially clueless.

Making repairs is a little too close to making *things*, to putting projects together, to assembling individual components into a useful or beautiful end result. Incompetence at one likely means a lack of skill at the other as well.

For one thing, I've always had trouble following instructions. Or, perhaps more accurately, I've been reluctant even to *look* at them. What's lacking, too, is an intuitive grasp of how things work, or should work, perhaps augmented by some actual study of the subject.

When you have trouble even finding the on-off switch of devices, the chance of a successful repair is slim indeed.

Surprisingly, I do have a small tool kit. I can even tell the difference between a regular screwdriver and a Phillips-head version. I've been known to wield a hammer without pounding my thumb in the process – though I might miss the nail completely now and then.

On the other hand, I'm far removed from Tim the Tool Man, as portrayed by Tim Allen on the old *Home Improvement* TV sitcom. I couldn't qualify to carry his tool belt.

Looking at a troubled device, some folks simply *know* what to do – or at least, what to try – to get a failed product working properly again. Or if the answer isn't immediately apparent, they are able to analyze the problem – and the solution – through reason and logic. Evidently, possible solutions just find their way into such talented folks' heads. We incompetents simply don't know anything – not even enough to blunder through a feeble, futile attempt.

One friend, for instance, is a scientist doing research in France. In addition to his vast expertise in his professional specialty, he's a fearless fixer of inoperative devices. When his DVD player stopped functioning, for example, he simply dove in and began to disassemble the unit, having deduced that it was likely a mechanical failure. Sure enough, a tiny component in the disc-carrying mechanism had worn down and could no longer do its job. Despite having no particular knowledge of DVD players or any similar device, Ken was able to repair the damage and restore the player to normal functionality.

Had it been up to me, I'd still be gazing at the player, with no idea how to begin. Or more likely, I'd be down at the store buying a new one – which is what's expected of us in today's non-repairable consumer society anyway.

Farmers, of course, must know how to fix just about everything. They can't call for help with every little thing that goes wrong. My good friend Al Spence, for instance, who raises cattle in rural Manitoba, is able to give his herd the necessary injections, assist at birthing calves, grow and distribute feed, till the soil, watch and analyze the weather, and be ready to repair and maintain all the equipment needed to keep even a small farm operating. I get exhausted and feel frightfully inferior just watching – or thinking about – him in action on a daily basis.

Two friends from my teenage years serve as prime examples of young people who were fearless in their attempts to repair anything. While still in high school, one of them worked as much as 80 hours a week repairing TVs, driving a company car to people's homes every afternoon and evening. While most young folks I knew were content with *listening* to music, these two started a business of their own, making tape recordings of concerts.

Repair Work

Household maintenance has long been a concern, because I'm so inept at all but the most elementary repair procedures and use of tools. Good thing I've always been an apartment dweller, able to request that someone else handle the more demanding tasks.

Even the simplest do-it-yourself installation has nearly always turned into an ordeal. When we lived in second-floor Chicago apartments, for example, it was necessary to remove our window air-conditioner as winter approached. Then, when spring drew near, it had to be reinstalled. Taking it out wasn't much of a problem, but reinserting the unit into the window spawned frightful reactions. Because the air-conditioner was heavy and poorly balanced, all I could do was worry: What if I lost my grip on the unit, and someone was standing right below our window? What if I dropped it right on someone's head?

Fortunately, year after year, I managed to keep the unit from slipping out of my grasp. But I never managed to assuage those fears of inadvertent disaster.

Not quite everyone around me realized how inept I was. Perceptions can differ sharply from reality. While working with a good friend who was trying to repair a tractor, during my visit to his farm, I tossed out a mild suggestion or two, based upon my modest knowledge of automobile technology. Later in the day, I was told, my friend's brother had commented on my particles of advice, stating that "he really knows his stuff" and helped a lot with the repair. Surprised? You bet. Little did he know how confused and unsure I'd been, standing on the sidelines and making what I considered to be a most minuscule contribution.

11

Making Things

Whenever I hear about home handymen whose basements contain a cornucopia of power and hand tools, I am mystified. These folks seem to *enjoy* making things. Assembling stuff. Creating a finished product out of basic parts.

More shocking yet, they seem to *finish* those projects. They even exhibit their handiwork, in their own homes or presented as gifts to friends and relatives.

Whenever I've tried to make or assemble anything, on the other hand, it's turned into an occasion for hand-wringing, head-shaking, and dangerous rising of blood pressure. Not to mention the possibility that the project in question may or may not ever get done.

Cooperative efforts at making things were, if anything, even worse. At some point in my early adult life, living in an apartment in the same building as my widowed mother, she stated that she wanted a small file cabinet. No problem there, except that the only ones we could find at a reasonable price had to be assembled. They were made of wood, and sold in kit form.

I should have known better.

My mother and I never worked together well. Just about every time we tried, we got on each other's nerves to the point of raised voices and fuming outbursts. So, we never should have attempted to assemble that file cabinet.

It seemed like such a simple project, though I was dismayed to discover that a considerable number of step-by-step instructions would have to be followed, in order to arrive at the wooden, two-drawer file cabinet pictured on the box.

If I'm to get anywhere with such a project, instructions had better be fully detailed, with no steps absent. I am able to follow directions, but I don't deduce what to do next on my own. Directions better not be totally pictorial, either. I respond well enough to words, but pictures, and especially icons, leave my mind drawing a blank.

Still, all that was involved, it appeared, would be lining up pieces, fitting the end of one chunk of wood into a slot cut into another, inserting and tightening screws. Nothing out of the ordinary. Nothing that should be beyond the qualifications even of an inept woodworker.

Looking back, all these years later, it sounds so simple. But not for my mother and myself. Joint efforts brought out the worst in both of us. Building that inconsequential file cabinet turned instead, once again, into an occasion for argument and obstinacy, much of it related to my difficulty in undertaking even the simplest build-it-yourself tasks.

Model cars were another example. From an early age, I fell for the flowing lines of classic and near-classic automobiles. Ever since I saw a photograph of cowboy actor Tom Mix's custom 1937 Cord, with steer horns mounted atop its hood, I was smitten. Having an opportunity to see the radical new Tucker automobile in person at Chicago's International Amphitheater in 1947, sitting atop my father's shoulders, further cemented my adoration of exquisite motorcars.

As a working-class teenager, of course, buying one of those elegant automobiles was out of the question. Sure, classic cars could sometimes be found in the Fifties for a few hundred dollars. But even that was beyond the reach of my wallet. So, like many car enthusiasts of that period, I turned to building plastic car models from over-the-counter kits. I remember them well: a 1941 Lincoln Continental. "Coffin-nose" 1937 Cord convertible. Auburn 835 Speedster. Cars that I loved, whether in person or in miniature.

Reality intruded on my love for fine automobiles in scale-model form, though. Somehow, no matter how painstaking my efforts at building them seemed to be – to my own eyes – the end result fell far short of the automotive beauty that I'd been expecting. Tiny glops of glue oozed out of the seams between mating panels. Pieces didn't line up quite right. Greasy fingerprints might be seen on the bodies and on the clear plastic windows. Paint jobs looked as if they'd been applied with a brush that had previously been used for cleaning bathtubs. Not only were my little display cars feeble examples of the modelmaker's craft, they deserved the lowest possible marks for neatness.

My difficulty with do-it-yourself kits actually had begun years earlier. Despite growing up in a working-class household, where money was always tight, Santa Claus was surprisingly generous to me as a child. Every December 25, I could expect a tantalizing selection of neatly-wrapped packages under the Christmas tree. Only a few of them would be socks or scarves, though my hung-up stocking might contain an orange. None of the parcels contained lumps of coal, either.

A lot of those Christmas gifts were kits of various sorts: boxes of intriguing items, ready to make stuff, to do experiments, to turn out projects. Not a single one of them ever worked out as hoped, or as promised by their makers. Many never worked at all; or, placed in my jurisdiction, yielded a product that would reduce any reasonable person to tears. Why? Sheer incompetence. My own. What else could it be?

Kits brought excitement into my life, when I first saw them. Until I actually opened the box, that is, and the certainty of yet another ordeal and ultimate failure erupted abruptly.

My photo darkroom kit, for instance, never resulted in a finished print that deserved to be shown to anyone, much less exhibited with pride. As I recall, they turned out smeary and faded-looking, regardless of the quality of the photo negative that was employed.

Chemistry set? Well, I didn't blow up our apartment building accidentally, but there were few, if any, fascinating, completed experiments to call attention to, either.

Whether starting with a kit or working from scratch, other kids would create craftsmanlike masterworks in wood or metal, presenting them with a flourish to their mother or girlfriend. Only an idiot would burden anyone with the paltry examples I was capable of producing. Mine came across as objects of shame, not pride, ready to be presented to the trash collector.

Part of it has always been lack of patience, coupled with an inability to stick with a project and be diligent about it. We incompetents just love to give up easily.

Unrealistic intentions also played a role, at times. At one point in my early teens, for instance, a friend and I decided we wanted to build a car. With a motor, able to be driven. Rather than steel, like real automobiles, our mini-sized vehicle would be made of wood. Largely because neither of us knew the first thing about taking on such a massive, overly ambitious project, it never got farther than laying out a chassis and sawing it into shape. How could it have? For months, that barely-begun foundation sat in the basement of my apartment building, awaiting further construction steps that never began. A typical conclusion to my inept, impractical, ultimately laughable imaginings.

At one point in my early life, when undergoing occupational therapy for a nervous condition, I was given a wooden bowl by the instructor/counselor. The bowl's inner and outer surfaces were coarse and rough. So, I was also handed a sheet of sandpaper. That would be my therapy: sanding that bowl, stroke after stroke after stroke.

In reality, that was a reasonable appraisal of my skill level. Yet, I couldn't even finish that bowl, which looked and felt just about as rough when I completed my sanding as it had at the beginning. A prime example of the true incompetent's lack of artistry and industry.

12

Small Talk

They invariably started with cocktails. As a non-drinker, I wasn't tempted at all by the open bar, which served anything you wanted without charge. I attended these events because I had to, not because I enjoyed them; and each occasion began with a sense of impending doom.

For nearly 20 years, as part of my job covering the automobile business as an independent journalist, I attended several dozen out-of-town media drive programs each year. Each was held at a lavish hotel or resort, with nearly all meals presented at top-end restaurants. Only once or twice in all those years did we stay at a modest hotel, on the level of, say, a Comfort Inn. I've been in more W and Four Seasons hotels than I could count, and dined in an endless stream of four-star restaurants.

For most of the journalists, those luxury accommodations and chef-prepared meals are a major perk. So are the cocktail receptions that precede each meal, with alcohol beverages of every sort flowing freely. One journalist even boasted of his experience at a European media program, where he had the "opportunity" to try the most expensive liquor the opulent hotel could offer: $400 a shot and, as always, paid for by the car company that covered his way to the event.

In addition to alcohol, the common denominator at these receptions is conversation. Journalists who see each other at similar events every other week greet their comrades like long-lost brothers, and mingle in clusters with the public-relations and auto-company people to engage in small talk. For the convivial types, it's a chance to talk freely, loosened by alcohol, with representatives of the company, who might reveal some highly-coveted secret information about a future product. (This rarely happens, of course; the executives are quite good at revealing exactly what they want to disclose, and nothing more.)

What might be termed posterior-bussing (using an old Chicago term, heard during the administration of the first Mayor Daley, back in the 1950s and 1960s) is an integral part of the small-talk process. Each side – journalist vs. company executives – is striving to impress the other, one way or another; and to flatter the opposition when appropriate.

For shy, introverted attendees such as myself, the receptions are something to be dreaded: essentially, the price one pays for the privilege of getting advance information about a new vehicle. Small talk, to me, is practically tantamount to getting one's teeth extracted, one by one, without benefit of anaesthetic. As a result, I'm the one standing quietly in the corner, or wandering the room aimlessly, clutching my Ginger Ale with a tightened fist.

Part of the problem is that I have little or nothing in common with most of the journalists, much less the company folks, most of whom think highly of themselves and the presumed importance of their work. Much of the talk is about cars, as expected. In fact, some of the participants seem to have little to say about anything that lacks a motor. But the topics do vary. Thankfully, politics seldom enters the conversation, either at the receptions or during the excruciatingly long dinners that follow. Regardless, for non-conversational guests, the minutes, the hours, pass like particularly lethargic turtles that lack even a tentative destination, but simply move ahead at an agonizingly slow pace.

Obviously, many of them – like many people in general – love the small talk. For the talkers, that's a major part of life. For the conversational incompetents, such occasions are something to be avoided when possible, and endured when there's no way out.

The difference between these groups is one of many ways in which people are split into two never-meshing camps:

1. Those who talk freely and easily about minor or major matters with those they hardly know.

2. Those for whom "small talk" is a dreaded ordeal, to be

evaded whenever possible.

Certainly, there are many other ways to separate people into "yea" and "nay" camps. But the ability to function orally in social settings makes an enormous difference in one's overall life. Those of us who cannot measure up are consigned to the periphery of social intercourse, whether for business or personal encounters.

Have you seen us? Sure you have, though you may not have noticed. We're the ones looking anguished and uncomfortable, painfully and glaringly alone, carrying a drink around as it were a bomb. Or, in some cases, guzzling down a string of them in the hope of instilling some artificial camaraderie. Slowly, tentatively, we may move a little closer to one of the clusters of conversationalists that have formed – but rarely close enough to be invited into the fold.

Not that we really *want* to participate. We simply know it's *expected*; therefore, we make a feeble attempt at fitting in. Most often, that attempt fails with a light, unnoticed thud. Therefore, we drift away again in search of yet another conversational possibility, certain that the next trial won't go any better.

Even those who know us fairly well seldom ask us to join. If they happened to be asked later on whether we were at this particular reception or cocktail hour, they'd probably scratch their heads, trying to recall any evidence of our presence. Largely because of our failure to communicate in small groups, we are the invisible ones.

Sometimes, we'll spy an empty chair or stool, and plop down quietly. Sitting serenely seems less abnormal than standing, clinging to that dreaded drink like a life preserver, without a word – encouraging or discouraging – slipping past our lips.

Inability to speak freely in groups – whether large or small gatherings – was nothing new. It was well established by my teenage years, persisting into early adulthood and beyond. One evening when in my early twenties, to take an extreme but all too familiar example, I visited an acquaintance at his parents' home. On that occasion, I was accompanied by a good friend who knew the other fellow far better than I did.

Despite the three of us having a few things in common, including have attended the same high school, I sat for what seemed like hours, if not days, in that basement rec room – utterly mute. Words flowed back and forth all evening, but not a peep came from my direction.

Quiet? From their perspective, I may as well have not been there at all. Or been dead, or unconscious.

So, what's the reason for our intense reticence? Why are we so socially inept, when so many of our brethren come across as boldly gregarious?

Shyness is clearly the obvious answer, but it's not a sufficient explanation. Some shy people, after all, are able to converse passably well in small groups, even though the words may be forced. Being bashful might have been the foundation for this asocial behavior, but it's often amplified by the simple fact of having nothing to say.

Not for us the glib, easy-flowing comments on anything and everything. While standing at the edge of a convivial group, chances are no statement, no question, no observation, no retort, will come to mind at all. Our brains stand empty for the duration, devoid of even the most elementary verbiage. An empty mind, even temporarily vacant, isn't likely to yield sparkling jewels of conversational treasure – or even a tarnished, subpar scrap of listless lore.

Aversion to small talk started when I was young and painfully shy (especially among girls), escalating in my teens. When I was 15 or so, I accompanied my father to the home of one of his brothers (my uncle). Rather than force me to hang around with the adults, they sent me to the basement, where my female cousin and her teenage friends were holding an impromptu party.

As soon as I descended the stairs to my cousin's lair, I could see that all the teenagers were in couples. Except for me, of course. No other stragglers. No loners.

More worrisome yet, they were wrapped in each other's embrace, and many remained in that position for much of the ensuing evening. It's possible that nobody even realized I was there, much less that I might be uncomfortable sitting quietly alone, with all that kissing and (presumably) petting going on. I wasn't about to look too closely at the intertwined physiques to discern exactly what they were doing.

(Younger or more sensitive readers may not be aware that extensive and intense kissing, in the olden days, was commonly known as "necking," while "petting" referred to touching certain body parts on the other person, without advancing to actual sexual activity. A joke in those days had a policeman spotting a couple engaged in rapturous embrace, which he feels he must put a stop to. "We're only necking," the frightened young man proclaims when caught in the act. "Well, put your neck back in your pants," the cop replies.)

When the tongue became involved in the act of kissing, the original mild activity became immediately known as "French kissing." (Those French people get credit for a lot of things, many of them quite pleasing to the senses.)

After what seemed like weeks, I excused myself, having uttered not a word to anyone, and climbed back upstairs to see if my father was finally ready to leave. Thankfully, he was. Better yet, neither he nor my uncle asked for a comment about the goings-on in the basement. Neither would ever know how a seemingly pleasant party for a flock of teens could be sheer torture for one who sat so far apart from the group. So much for my skills as a partygoer.

On another occasion, a few years later, I went with a close friend to visit a fellow he'd known well in high school. I'd known him slightly, and envied – even admired – the fact that he'd driven a motorcycle regularly and owned a series of interesting old automobiles – in stark contrast to the chain of humdrum clunkers that I drove in these days. Enroute to his basement for an evening of chatting, I learned that his father was a labor organizer. This, at a time when I was immersed in study of the union movement, and hoped to find a career of some sort in that field.

In other words, we seemed to have a few things in common, so conversation shouldn't have been a problem.

Wrong! For what seemed like weeks, but was actually an hour

or two, I sat rigidly in my chair, tense to the point of immobility, uttering not a single word while the two of them talked and talked about a variety of subjects. Anyone observing that trio would have assumed that I was mute, or perhaps even mentally disabled. I may have learned a lot from hearing their words, but I contributed absolutely nothing to the evening, apart from a sense of unbearable awkwardness.

Even public speaking, something I dreaded all my life, turned out to be easier than chatting with acquaintances, as we'll see in Chapter 29. Once in a great while during my career as an automotive journalist, I was asked to submit to a radio or TV interview, or to participate in a panel broadcast on radio. Oddly, I turned out to be better at *being* interviewed than conducting interviews, though in each case it was as if another person was doing the talking, while I watched from the sidelines. The panel discussion went tolerably well, until the moment when the moderator asked a question and pointed his finger directly at me, as if daring me to speak. I couldn't. I turned totally mute, having no idea what the question was, much less being able to provide an answer.

Not until I became a sporadic guest on a locally-produced but nationally-viewed TV show did my hitherto-unknown capabilities as a speaker to a wide audience spring to the surface.

Later in life, I did manage to acquire a shred of ability to chat with one – or maybe two – individuals. With some driving partners, in the course of my work as an automotive journalist, I've become almost a veritable "Chatty Kathy," blurting out all sorts of details about myself. On those occasions, too, it's as if some alternate rendition of myself is chatting away, while the "real" me simply watches and listens in amazement.

Even today, though, put me at a dinner table set for six or eight, and it's a sure bet that few, if any, words will be emanating from my corner that evening.

13

Sex and Romance

Who would ever admit to being incompetent at sex? Or romance and all that involves? To hear most people – notably males – tell it, they're all stallions in the bedroom and Don Juans when enroute to each erotic encounter. They look back upon a string of conquests in their past and, often as not, a row of eager, potential partners in the present who'd like nothing more than to lure them to bed.

Performance? They're ready and able to do what's expected, and to last as long as it takes.

At least, that's what they believe, and what they enjoy relating to male friends. Figures on the number of men making use of erectile-dysfunction medications and assorted enhancement measures, on the other hand, appear to tell a rather different story of male sexual prowess.

My own story is more basic. From an early age, I've simply not been adept at anything related to sex, romance, or physical relationships. There. I've said it. I've admitted the inadmissible, and the sky hasn't fallen.

Back in high school years, when everyone around me appeared to be dating and getting somewhere with girls, I was a non-participant. No dates, no hugs, no kisses, apart from one or two odd, brief, and uncomfortable teenage boy/girl encounters. And certainly nothing more ambitious than that.

Why was I so totally out of it? Was I hideously repulsive? Did I invariably provoke reactions of disgust and distaste in the female populace?

Evidently not, since in later years I did manage to interest a female or two – including one who became my wife.

No, the answer was simple: I was frightfully, morbidly petrified of girls. Any girls. All girls. The very idea of talking to a girl filled me with dread. I couldn't even imagine casually walking up to a female person and trying to initiate a conversation. How other teenage boys could do so – and do it nonchalantly – was a total mystery.

Tongue-tied? More like a giant weight attached to my tongue, making it impossible to utter more than an occasional grunt or wheeze. My inability with the young ladies gave new meaning to words like "shy" and "bashful."

Early on, my romantic life had looked a bit more promising. At age ten I had my first date, taking the girl who lived upstairs to see Humphrey Bogart and Walter Huston in *Treasure of the Sierra Madre* at our nearest neighborhood theater, the Music Box. During one particularly intense scene in that film, when one of the prospectors turns over a big rock, an iguana suddenly appears. Girls in the audience screamed at the sight, my date among them. As I recall, she may even have grabbed my hand for solace. Things were looking up.

But not for long. Soon, the boys who hung out at our urban corner began to razz me about my romantic exploits. "Jimmy's got a girlfriend!" they'd cry out, repeatedly. Not wanting to be pointed out by my peers in any way, much less made fun of, I gave in to their taunts. That first date was the last one for many years to come, interrupted by only a handful of tentative outings.

To this day, I must admit – sixty-plus years later – I can't watch *Treasure of the Sierra Madre* (my favorite film ever, which I've probably seen a hundred times) without thinking of Joyce, my very first, if short-term, girlfriend.

It didn't help that I attended a huge all boys' public high school in Chicago. Yes, that concept sounds quaint now, and that school began to admit girls a while after I graduated. But in the 1950s, single-sex high schools, public and private, weren't uncommon at all.

All I ever saw, then, every day – apart from the teachers – were boys. Four thousand boys. Somehow, that lack of feminine presence failed to impede the romantic progress of most of my friends and acquaintances. They had no hesitation about going to events held at the co-ed or all-girl high schools, or simply striking up relationships right on the street.

My God, I thought at the time. Those other guys actually are able to talk with girls! Not only talk, but wind up romantically involved with a few of them. Or in some cases, to hear them tell it, a lot of them.

Ah, but then came the Prom. Foolishly, after considerable consternation, I decided that I "should" go. It was virtually obligatory: the "thing to do," in one's final year of high school. I'd regret it all my life if I stayed home. Wouldn't I?

At age 16, a graduating Senior at Lane Tech High School, I was acquainted with practically no girls at all. Certainly none who could be considered prospects as a Prom date. With one exception. I'd actually exchanged a word or two with the cute, friendly 15-year-old girl next door. Rather than spring the Prom question on her without warning, I gathered up my full supply of courage – a minuscule amount, to be sure – and asked her out to a movie, as a prelude to popping the *big* question. Amazingly, she said yes.

This was only a short time before the event. For weeks, several friends at school, aware of my difficulty in finding a partner for the dance, had tried to find a date for me. One evening, I crawled into the back seat of one friend's 1950 Oldsmobile, so a group of us could head over to a certain Woolworth's five-and-ten-cent store. Why? Because a girl they thought might be a prospect for me worked at the store, and would be clocking out soon.

When she slipped into the front seat, I was impressed with their choice. She was more than passably cute, in the very familiar Chicago ethnic way. During our short drive, though, neither she nor I said a word to the other. Clearly, she knew the reason for our forced encounter that evening. After she got out of the car, in front of her home, nobody said anything about what might have been considered a pre-blind date. No one said a word later, either. The message was abundantly clear: she wasn't interested. Naturally, I couldn't blame her.

Having struck out so dismally once, without having even swung lightly, the girl next door sounded even more tempting. So, I was both excited and relieved when she agreed to that movie date.

More than that, of course, I was frightened. What would I say to her at the movies? Was I expected to hold her hand at some point? Try something more assertive afterward? Or was it okay to keep my distance, perhaps letting her believe I was just too gentlemanly to make an improper move.

To say our movie date was quiet and uneventful would be quite an understatement. I've no idea what movie we saw, and probably didn't even know at the time. I wasn't concentrating on the screen. All I could think of was her presence. How could I help being overloaded with tension, sitting so close to a budding 15-year-old female who'd already developed all the graceful curves and contours of feminine allure. Especially when I saw myself not as a dedicated man-in-the-making, but as a scared little boy trying in vain to take a forbidding step toward adulthood. Though the vision of such intimacy sent my teenage mind into a tailspin, that date was destined to be as chaste as a boy-girl pairing could be: as if we were brother and sister.

Despite saying little in the course of our tense afternoon session at the North Center Theater, I did manage to blurt out an invitation to the Prom as I dropped her off at home. Without hesitation, she said yes.

How could that be? Why would she agree to accompany an all-out dork to such a major occasion in teenage lives? There's an easy answer to that one, I believe. In that part of Chicago, attending a Lane Tech Prom was a feather in a young girl's cap, a sought-after goal, a high mark on her romantic scoreboard, no matter who the hapless escort happened to be.

Prior to the Prom, like all the other boys, I made a trip downtown to the Gingiss Brothers store, which catered to students in need of formal wear. For the first (and last) time in my life, I rented a tuxedo. White coat and all the *accouterments*, including a pair of fancy shoes.

I also bought the requisite corsage that was part of the mating ritual, to be mounted when I picked her up at her home for our memorable evening. Instead of the kind of corsage worn on the wrist, however, I'd picked the type that had to be pinned to the top of the young lady's strapless gown.

Well, I wasn't about to undertake *that* intimate task. Certainly not in her living room, with her parents standing right there. I was only too aware of what obviously lay directly beneath that upper portion of her frilly dress, and couldn't allow myself to think of such matters. Her mother, therefore, actually wound up applying the pin that would hold the fragile flower in place.

Exiting her residence, we headed for the street, and stepped into our conveyance for the occasion: my 1948 Chevrolet coupe, faded maroon, complete with rustouts at the base of each door. Other boys in my high-school class had flashy convertibles or semi hot-rods, glistening brightly, their dual exhausts rumbling energetically. I had an old wreck – the first of a long line of jalopies that would constitute my automotive ownership history.

Fortunately, the Chevrolet made it to the Medinah Country Club, some 20 miles west of Chicago, without faltering. Spending an evening at such an elegant retreat was another "first" for me, and almost certainly for her. We even tried dancing once or twice. My stiff, leaden movements, like those of a wooden soldier slowly making his way back from a devastating war, made a mockery of the music supplied by the orchestra. They deserved better – and got it, from many of the other Prom-goers, who were eager to display their talents with the latest dance steps.

Photos were taken of the two of us. She looked absolutely lovely, a gently smiling teenage queen. In stark contrast, I gave the impression of a cross between a skinny, brainless scarecrow and some inappropriate interloper who'd joined the festivities as a crazed impostor, and would likely be hauled away soon by the authorities.

No recollection remains of the dinner we presumably enjoyed afterward at Mangam's Chateau, a popular and rather classy suburban dining establishment. I'd never set foot in such a place in my life, and wouldn't again for many years to come, until I became a traveling auto journalist. We shared a table with two good friends and their dates, who'd arrived together in a separate car, a 1947 Oldsmobile 98 borrowed from one of their brothers.

No doubt, some of the boys managed to bring along a little alcoholic refreshment, to accompany the soda pop served by the waiters to this crowd. At that point in my life, I'd never tasted alcohol. A year later, I'd be well on my way to becoming a full-fledged alcoholic. But on this occasion, no drinks were present at our dining table.

As we departed the Chateau after dinner, the parking attendant couldn't start my rusty, ragged 1948 Chevrolet coupe. Therefore, I had to amble ignominiously over to the parking area myself to get it fired up, collecting my Prom date at the front door as if I were a taxi driver.

Even my attempt to salvage my tattered reputation a bit by "peeling out" of the driveway fell short. The goal was to gun the engine hard, snap the clutch and cause the back wheels to spin, thereby "burning rubber" on the driveway pavement. Rather than the screech and stench of rubber that I'd hoped to expel as I roared toward the street, my balding tires eked out only a feeble chirp, noticed by no one. It was a fitting departure, signifying the final gasp of a deteriorated gala evening, and an attempt to fit into the crowd for once in my teenage life.

Back in Chicago at her front gate, despite my hidden longing – which I'd somehow managed to hold in check all evening – no kiss, no hug ended the evening. Certainly nothing beyond that. Not even a quick peck on the cheek, in either direction. Why, we didn't even exchange a firm handshake. She knew only too well how terrified I was, I believe; and to her credit, she managed a graceful exit without the usual brief displays of adolescent affection. Our parting, after the biggest event of the high-school season, was more like a nonchalant wave and a less-than-hearty, tossed-off "see ya."

Memories of that disastrous evening clouded my conception of romantic encounters for years to come. Now, sixty years later, a sense of dread still creeps down my back whenever I think of that celebratory event. Ironically, not so long afterward, I heard that my teenage Prom date was married and had a baby.

After high school and into early college years, the romantic scene failed to improve. Though in later life I might appear more poised on the surface than I had during teenage years, and into my early twenties, inside I was the same frightened, terminally shy and awkward dork who'd forced himself to attend that high-school Prom. Through the decades, from my teens all the way into senior-citizenhood, I invariably lacked even a shred of self-confidence and self-assuredness.

On those rare occasions when I did muster sufficient courage to establish contact with a person of the female persuasion, I made some unfortunate choices, winding up in a couple of relationships that should never have happened. Once sexual activity entered the picture, my frenzied brain went into a tailspin. Though incredibly intense, those early sexual experiences took place with an utterly inappropriate partner, and/or in an awkward setting. Therefore, all that biological excitement was in effect wasted, turning instead into guilt and remorse that lasted the rest of my days and greatly impaired my future sex life.

Jealousy reared its ugly head, too, doubtless because getting to the point of physical contact had been such a battle that I wanted to cling to it with a passion beyond normal, even for a young male. Before long, any pleasure derived from a physical encounter on any level would be stopped in its tracks by waves of guilt, coupled with an intensifying urge to hold on tight and never let go.

Not exactly the tone one hopes for to get a bit of fun out of a relationship. Though exciting and stimulating in the customary ways of the teenager and young adult, these sessions weren't really fun at all. In fact, they set the stage for a lifetime in which sex, when it existed at all, would invariably be dominated by guilt and worry.

We think of Jewish Guilt, Catholic Guilt, and a few other religious-related versions. I belonged to none of those groups, but had no doubt that I could match each of them, item for item, on the guilt scale.

Making matters vastly worse was one session of grappling that took place in a car, late at night, in a public park in wintertime Chicago. Achieving a state of partial undress, what do we see but a policeman at the car window, shining a flashlight into the car. Quickly straightening ourselves, we unlocked the door, since it was clear that he was not about to accept a rejection of his plea for entry. So there he was, smiling vapidly in the back seat, mulling over what to do about us. Since I was never a fan of cops in the first place – a common opinion in working-class Chicago – my heart was racing madly from the effort to answer his questions calmly.

But why wasn't he carting us off to the station, if that was his goal? Well, this was Chicago, in an earlier time. Gradually, it became clear that he didn't much care what we'd been doing, or intended to do, in that front seat. He wanted a payoff. A bribe. At that moment, my wallet was close to empty, but sitting on the ledge beneath the back window was a gun. No, not the kind of gun used to stick up people. I wasn't a budding criminal. It was an air pistol, which I'd won in a raffle and stupidly tossed into the back seat of the car.

That was good enough for him. When he picked up the pistol, I thought I was really in for it: that I'd be charged with unlawful possession of a weapon. Air pistols weren't illegal, but everyone knew that the Chicago police weren't above adjusting the rules.

Fortunately, a light dawned in my head. "You can have it," I said to him. Grinning even more brightly, he agreed to the gift and, with an almost cheery farewell, exited from the back seat. He was gone; but the fright he'd caused never went away. From then on, any sexual encounter, however mild, would be tarnished by the memory of that night in the park.

Plenty of other reasons for sexual incompetence came to light in those days, some of them physical. In addition to the typical concern about inadequate size, there was the issue of – let's be blunt – what we'll call a premature conclusion. This phenomenon was doubtless due, at least in part, to the tension created whenever

I was in the company of a possibly willing female.

If lack of confidence wasn't enough to restrain any romantic impulses, two other obstacles invariably rattled around in my head: fear of disease (even in that pre-AIDS era), and dread of pregnancy.

Mainly, though, the sexual problems have all been mental, which leads us to the activity that cannot be overlooked: self-stimulation. Having participated in this ritual since the age of eight or so, I should have become the world's most capable practitioner of what Ignatius J. Reilly referred to as his "hobby." (For readers unfamiliar with the name, Ignatius was the memorably iconoclastic antihero in the great novel *A Confederacy of Dunces*, which won a Pulitzer Prize in 1981, years after the suicide of the author, John Kennedy Toole.)

Pre-adolescent incidences of mild homosexual contact with a pair of same-age boys didn't help prepare me for a heterosexual future, either. Years later, I was amazed to discover that such experiences were far from uncommon during childhood. But the damage had been done. In addition to placing a fog over contact with females, they instilled a fear of homosexuals that persisted for years. As expected, too, that was coupled with a fear that I might actually *be* one, even though I had no lustful interest in persons of the same sex. (In this era of rapidly-growing acceptance of gay life, fear of homosexuality sounds so ancient; but in the 1950s, being perceived as a "queer" or "fag" was an assertion to be avoided at all costs.)

Not until my early twenties was the uncertainty about my own sexual identity quashed, thankfully preventing actual homophobia from developing. One fellow I knew slightly was in a car with my group of friends, and heard me say I sometimes wondered if I were actually, secretly, homosexual. "You're not," he declared, emphatically. And as we quickly realized, he would know. Unbeknownst to the rest of us, he was unabashedly gay himself. Closeted, in the manner that was the rule in the early Sixties, but 100-percent homosexual.

Years later, too, when I learned that various colleagues in the journalism business were gay, any vestigial hints of homophobia faded away fully. I can't say I became tolerant, because I always had been – unlike most of the males in the working-class Chicago neighborhood of my childhood, sad to say. In those days, taunts suggesting that one might have "queer" tendencies served as part of the currency of youthful male bonding.

On a broader level of causation, my self-image scored down among the bottom-feeders. That impression was stimulated in large measure by a different sort of encounter, on a bus when I was 15, riding with a close friend. As we were exiting the bus, a teenage girl rudely called out to us: "Goodbye, ugly."

That was enough for me. For years – indeed, decades – to come, I would perceive myself as an ugly man whom no woman would ever want to be around. Even when, over the years, an occasional female expressed an interest in me, her attentions did nothing to erase that perception of ugliness.

Oddly, several years later, before he died at age 25, that friend told me he'd assumed that the girl's cruel remark was aimed at *him*. And it had a deleterious impact upon him as well. Those who blurt out hateful barbs might never realize how long-lasting the impact of their hurtful words can be. Then again, maybe they do. Still, her stabbing words were probably forgotten within seconds after leaving her mouth, only to stick firmly within the minds of two painfully insecure boys.

Until meeting and eventually marrying my wife, in my early 30s, every relationship – and there weren't many, believe me – ended in disaster in some form. Each one added an extra layer of guilt. Each was lacking in joy, but overloaded with arguments and tension. Looking back, it's a wonder that I've ever been able to gain any pleasure at all from sexual or romantic activities.

Family matters certainly didn't help, either. My father was a gregarious man, fond of women, easily able to strike up conversations. His only advice to me about women was simple: "Wear a rubber." (For the edification of younger readers, that's what we called condoms in ancient times.)

Toss in the fact that after moving from the city to the outlying suburbs in the mid-1950s, he spent most evenings after work lounging on the couch reading a book, and it's a wonder that I was able to have any sex life at all later on. Why? Because during the last few years before his death at age 52, he did his lounging in the nude, his abundant male organ in plain sight – ignoring the picture window a few feet away.

Up until then, he'd given no apparent indication of a leaning toward nudity or naturism. And it's a sure bet that my conservative mother, always worried about what the neighbors might think, was not happy about this freewheeling practice. Nor was I, partly because his leisurely flaunting of his physique practically begged for comparison with my own minuscule male unit.

Many years later, when I finally forced myself to ask the woman who became my wife for a date, in 1973, I had been without female companionship for seven years. And my last relationship, a several-month parody of romance, had turned into an unmitigated disaster of accusations and paranoia.

That's seven years lacking not only sex with another person, but the hugs and kisses, cooings and warm talks, that accompany such couplings. I was a solitary, isolated person, presumably surrounded by copulating couples and amorous attentions, well aware that the average 16-year-old was vastly more sexual active that I'd ever been, or ever would be.

Ironically, that seven-year period of celibacy roughly coincided with the peak of the fabled "Sexual Revolution" that began in the Sixties. During that time span, when I was a young adult, I didn't have even a casual date; hardly a conversation with a woman, for that matter.

My place in that period of sexual liberation would best be described by the title of a book depicting the era: *Start the Revolution Without Me*. Though tales of rampant sexual activity were reported throughout the nation, I neither participated in it, nor observed much of it. The possibility of finding a romantic companion – or a sexual partner – was just as slim as it had been before, in the

Sex and Romance

puritanical Fifties and early Sixties.

Improved contraception and the rise of the counterculture changed the social mores pertaining to sex; or so it seemed. All around, we were informed constantly, a barrage of sexual activity was taking place. Everyone was doing it. Free love was in the air. Girls were willing, eager, uninhibited.

Exactly where these girls could be found, however, was far less clear to the uninitiated.

In those days, I didn't patronize the kinds of places and events where young people met and "hooked up." Most evenings, I slunk into neighborhood taverns, sitting alongside middle-aged and older gentlemen who were there to drink, not establish connections. Opportunities to meet a woman who might be seeking a relationship were rarities, at best. Besides, when the revolution and my seven-year stretch of relationship-free life were well underway, I ceased drinking completely, fearful that my excessive consumption since age 17 would soon kill me. I stopped cold, and never touched alcohol again.

I wasn't even *acquainted* with any young women who might be available or interested. Where did others find partners, anyway, I often wondered. I worked at home as an independent freelance writer, seeing colleagues only occasionally and briefly; so workplace romance was out. I met almost no women "on the job," beyond a brief hello now and then. I took almost no classes following graduation from college in 1964; and if I had, would still have lacked the confidence and courage to approach a potentially available female person.

Neither did I belong to any groups. My evenings were typically spent drinking in solitude. Unable to dance in either slow or rapid tempo, establishments with dance floors were off-limits, except for those wooden pallets that stood in front of the jukebox in some cocktail lounges.

Like other romantic incompetents, I observed the Sexual Revolution from the fringe. But not quite always. On one occasion during this period, I stumbled into an opportunity for a threesome, of all things, with friends who had been casually dating for some time. While the three of us were hanging out in the fellow's bedroom one evening, she announced, without warning: "I'm going to take off my clothes." And proceeded to do exactly that. All of them.

Positioning herself on the floor, she gave the impression that a session with either of us might not be inadmissible. Perhaps both of us, one at a time.

Dispensing with clothing myself, I hit the floor next to her and hesitantly began a frenzied approach. By now, several years had passed since my last sexual encounter of any sort. Much as I wanted to go further, I just couldn't get comfortable. So, I left the floor to the two of them and eased myself out of the room – without my pants. Which caused a bit of a stir when the male partner's roommate returned home, shortly thereafter.

Years earlier, an even more bizarre opportunity had emerged: for a *foursome*, of all things. Unfortunately, that encounter turned nasty in a hurry. After playing strip poker for a while, the two girls leaped up from their chairs and quickly wound up in bed, nude and presumably available. Here too, I started out enthusiastically; but in my drunken state, jealousy and guilt quickly rose to the surface, prompting an outburst that instantly killed the mood for romance in all of us. I still regret my outlandish behavior on what could have been a most memorable night.

14

Making Friends

On holidays, on the job, anywhere at all, we see people forming friendships. Some are destined to last a long while. Others are sure to be fleeting. But they're friendships, nonetheless.

Being a terminally shy person all my life, until fairly recently I could barely even *imagine* striking up a personal conversation with a stranger, whether at a bar, in a café, at work, or in a class. Now and then, it's happened, resulting in some rewarding acquaintances – as well as plenty of awkward encounters. Most often, though, unless the other party took the initiative, little more than a bashful, hesitant "Hello" was likely to emanate from my lips.

Discerning readers might already guess that I've always been a loner. Yes, the kind invariably referred to with suspicion whenever some heinous crime has been committed and the police are looking for the latest serial killer.

As described previously in the chapter on Small Talk, even a *little* talk is usually beyond my capabilities.

Across the table on a train, with a seatmate on a bus or plane, my preference would be to *avoid* any conversation. Given a chance to sit alone, I'll grab it. In hotels or at tourist destinations, I never make friends or acquire acquaintances. When a trip is over, there's no one whom I ever expect to see or hear from again.

Other people see these situations as opportunities to be sought out and savored. For me, they're occasions of nervousness and tension, worrying about what to say next and whether that last statement sounded ridiculously stupid.

Growing up in working-class Chicago in the 1940s and early 1950s, I always had several friends. Most were kids who lived in the same apartment building as my family, or who resided a few doors away and hung out on the same corner of two side streets that I frequented. We might call it the Janssen Avenue group, though its members resided only on a short stretch of that street or around the corner on Byron Avenue -- up to just past the alley, in each case. Anyone living beyond that point wasn't likely to be part of our little group.

Oddly, though, that small group of childhood friends almost invariably included at least one outsider, who likely lived farther away. Typically, the most notorious outcast in the class or around the neighborhood. Why? Did I consciously seek out what might be called "dumb" friends? Probably, though some of them seemed to gravitate toward me, rather than the reverse. I'd say it was a signal that I saw myself as headed in that very same direction, turning into an outcast who didn't really belong anywhere.

No point being coy here: in elementary school, I was among the smartest kids in class – as measured by grades, at least. But one of those offbeat childhood friends was likely to be near the opposite end of the intellectual spectrum: older than average, and frankly, not very bright.

As is often the case, starting high school meant leaving old friends behind, and striving to become part of a new group. Numerically speaking, my group of friends declined to a small handful as cliques formed and special-interest clubs separated students from their peers. By sophomore year, I was part of a group of four who sat together at lunch every day. A curious quartet it was, and one that would change my life – mostly for the better.

One was the odd man out – a kid who practically defined the word nebbish, or nerd, or misfit. Unlike misfits I'd known before (and since), though, Terry seemed comfortable in his apart-from-the-pack role. He made no attempt at all to fit into anyone's group, and gave no evidence of being bothered by other students' unflattering opinions of him.

Edward occupied a social status at the other end of the scale, benefitting from the kind of good looks that induced young girls to swoon – and to overlook his pockmarked face, a result of the acne that ran rampant in those days. He also straddled an unusual line, exhibiting the demeanor and tone of an urban tough guy; but underneath, a smart kid who was no slouch in the academic area. Not only did he have his own car in early high-school years, but it was a flashy Chrysler convertible.

Then there was Perry, who came across as the oldest, most mature, most sophisticated teenager you could ever imagine. Having grown up in a tough neighborhood of Chicago, he was fully accepted by the ruffian elements at Lane Technical High School. By virtue of my friendship with him, Perry helped make it possible for me to survive that period of my life, without becoming a victim of bullying. Perpetrators of bullying behavior evidently thought twice before picking me out as a potential butt of their taunts or antics, based at least in part on the fact that I was regularly seen in the company of two young gentlemen who, in the parlance of the Chicago mob, might be referred to as "connected."

At the same time, Perry changed my life, transforming me from a teenager with working-class sensibilities and views of the world into a semi-sophisticate who could appreciate the finer points of life. Without his tutelage and encouragement, I would never have taken an interest in classic music, in opera, in "foreign" movies, in serious literature, in any sort of intellectual pursuits. No friend has ever made such a positive difference in my life. Later in life, on the other hand, no one I've known has ever proven to be so elusive as Perry, so strange in behavior, so difficult to understand, so prone to conspiracy theories, so ready to see himself as above the law and many of the rules that restrict our everyday actions.

Moving into young-adult life, I continued to gravitate toward people who stood apart from the pack. Some were unique in favorable, intriguing ways. Others were just – well, different, in ways that lacked charm and grace. One or two were borderline criminals. Even when I realized immediately that these were folks to be avoided, not sought out, often as not I'd extend a hand of tepid friendship regardless. Few ever became actual friends, but their presence, even if short-lived, cast a questionable shadow upon my developing personality.

On one dark wintry night, for instance, I found myself in the car of a friend of the fellow who was, at the time, closest to being my best friend. Why? All these years later, I still can't answer that question. Martin was a door-to-door magazine salesman, traveling the country, pushing anyone unwise enough to answer their doorbell to buy magazine subscriptions they didn't need, and probably didn't want. Having worked briefly for a similar company myself – unsuccessfully – during a time of desperation, I should have realized immediately that a successful salesperson in that field was someone to steer clear of. Yet here I was, in the passenger seat of Martin's brand-new DeSoto hardtop, roaring down Chicago's Clark Street – which still held streetcar tracks – at something close to 80 miles an hour (triple the legal limit).

It should be noted that in my teen years and early Twenties, I was not averse to fast driving. In fact, I'm ashamed to admit how much of it I'd done, often while intoxicated and behind the wheel of decrepit, dangerous cars that belonged in the scrapyard. Yet, even I knew – could instantly see – that Martin's prowess at the wheel, even at legal speeds, fell short of skillful. Rather than insist on getting out of that car, though, I endured his maniacal hurtling through the urban streets until we wound up at an all-night restaurant for coffee. Not much time passed before I realized that he and I had absolutely nothing in common, nothing to talk about, no reason to be pursuing any sort of connection, much less even the most hesitant, impersonal friendship. Thankfully, following that seemingly endless night, I never saw him again.

So, why was I there in the first place, spending hours with someone I didn't like, and would soon be glad to be rid of? Nothing more than the normal urge for companionship and conversation. Sure, he was a maniac and a creep, with whom I shared nothing whatsoever. But I had nowhere else to go that night (or most nights). No one else to see, or talk with. Nothing to do at all. For a short time, being in this creepy, high-risk fool's company seemed better than nothing. It wasn't.

Why do I even remember that night, more than half a century later? Nothing memorable or noteworthy happened. Nothing to regret, nothing that needed to be forgotten. It was utterly uneventful: just another way to pass the time. But when your supply of friends, and even acquaintances, is sharply limited, it's all too easy to fall in with undesirable people, simply because they agree to spend time with you. All the more so when none of the people you consider to be friends qualify as a buddy, in even the broadest sense of the word. Moving firmly into adulthood, the number of those who might be perceived as a pal shrunk from nearly none down to absolute zero.

As we'll see in the next chapter, not all long-lasting relationships are benign. Even a person who was once regarded as a friend can turn out to be something quite different, possibly even leading to a hefty dose of guilt, shame, and/or regret.

College is typically presumed to be the time of life when social relationships gain serious currency and lifelong friends are made. Could be, but not for me. That's partly because my college education began in night school, soon shifting into a stint at the Chicago branch of the University of Illinois. Since the mid-1960s, the Chicago branch of that institution has been a conventional university campus. But in the late Fifties, when I first attended, classes were held along Navy Pier: a mile-long slab of pavement jutting into Lake Michigan, previously used as a warehouse but converted to a institution of higher learning after World War II, to serve the needs of returning veterans whose studies were subsidized by the G.I. Bill of Rights. A more impersonal setting for study could hardly be imagined.

Obviously, despite the dull surroundings and the fact that this university branch was known as a "serious" school for modest-income urbanites, most students managed to strike up relationships during their semesters at "the pier." I was not among them. Not only were no lifelong friendships formed, but I don't recall exchanging more than an occasional hello with any other student.

On registration day, for example, I was assigned to share a locker with an attractive young woman, admittedly prompting – momentarily – a lascivious thought or two. In reality, after checking out the locker once, I never used it again; and of course, never saw that lovely young lady again.

Not much changed in the social-life department when I headed down to the central part of the state, to finish my last three semesters at the main campus of the University of Illinois. Positioned at the junction between the adjacent cities of Champaign and Urbana, this was a full-fledged university campus, complete with dormitories, graduate schools, bars and hangouts that catered to the massive student population.

In fact, the U of I was a traditional-type "Big 10" campus. Not that the latter meant much to me, as a total non-sports fan. Had I been asked where the football stadium was located on campus, I'd have been stumped – even after attending that institution for three semesters, until graduation with a B.A. degree.

Except for my roommates in a series of off-campus houses jointly rented by as many as five of us, I had no friends at the university, and few acquaintances, during the year and a half I spent there. Once again, I was strictly one of those loners you hear about in sensationalistic newspaper stories.

Two of my roommates were actually guys I knew back in Chicago. Working at the university library yielded a couple of acquaintances, including the head librarian – until she chastised me in no uncertain terms because patrons had complained that I had alcohol on my breath. Yes, I spent much of my collegiate life drinking. Not at parties, as depicted in countless movies about university life, but at home. Alone. Typically, in my room.

Any hope for a normal social life on-campus evaporated in the aftermath of a disastrous party at our house. What began as a singular exception to my lack of friendly encounters with persons of the female gender ended, a few hours later, as a sad, drunken debacle.

Although I'd anticipated staying in my room upstairs through the evening, an unusually friendly young woman suddenly poked her head into my doorway, asking if I intended to come downstairs to join the festivities. Practically before I knew it, the two of us were in the living room clinging to each other, ostensibly dancing but in reality barely moving across the carpet, as she ran her fingers through my hair.

For a solitary, isolated person who seldom spoke to anyone, whether on-campus or off, this turn of events was nothing short of heavenly. All the more so, when I suddenly brought forth a particle of courage and asked if she cared to accompany me to a Law School party a few weeks off – and she said yes! Evidently, my fortunes were changing fast in the socialization area. Only a couple of weeks before, I'd started classes at the Law School, which was offered as an option for senior year. Now, I was about to become a participant in the casual realm of legal studies as well, mingling with serious students of the legal profession.

Not so fast. As was invariably the case in those days, I was consuming plenty of alcohol during that party. As dawn loomed, for reasons I couldn't begin to explain, I – who had no religious affiliation of any sort and hadn't set foot in a house of worship since my Confirmation at age 12 – proposed that several of us who remained in party mode attend services at the nearby Catholic church. Trouble is, I also proposed driving there in my decrepit 1948 Hudson. Within minutes, after making what was evidently a ragged turn onto another side street, I was in the hands of the police, headed for court on what could have been a drunken-driving charge. (For reasons unknown, the judge reduced it to a lesser charge, which, months later, was dismissed.)

Meanwhile, the two girls in the car wound up in trouble at their dormitories, and I couldn't face the one who'd agreed to go to the Law School party. Shamefully, rather than tell her myself that I had to cancel that date, I asked one of my roommates to do it. Not long afterward, when facing the Law School's disciplinary committee myself, I was reproached more for my unconscionable lack of civil behavior toward that girl, after the incident, than for the incident itself. And deservedly so. My actions were driven by fear and panic, but were nonetheless unprincipled. Of the many regrets in my life, virtually begging for a do-over, that one stands near the pinnacle.

At the end of that first semester, I dropped out of Law School and returned to a conventional Liberal Arts curriculum for my final semester as a university student. My short-lived legal career was over, long before it began.

Would I have been better off – more socialized and socially adept – if I'd lived in a dormitory rather than off-campus with older students? Probably not, since I was a couple of years older than the average undergrad myself. I finished college in spurts – three sessions over a seven-year period – rather than the normal four consecutive years.

Of course, another factor enters into the picture, based upon my sense of inferiority and living as an outsider: the feeling that I didn't *deserve* to have real, normal friends. That feeling was amplified at the age of 22, when the symptoms of what was diagnosed as "anxiety and panic reaction" that had plagued me for the previous five years reached a crescendo. Unable to cope any longer, I checked myself – voluntarily – into a public mental hospital: the brand-new Illinois State Psychiatric Institute, on the near west side of Chicago.

Except for the 3.5 months I spent at the Institute, I never lived in a communal setting: military, college dormitory, group work. Most of my young adult life was spent living alone, in a long string of furnished rooms, interspersed with a couple of hotels.

Though frightening at first, checking into the Institute and living in a group setting soon turned into a revelation. For the first few weeks of voluntary commitment, due to anxiety and shyness, I was isolated from the group at large. But then, I suddenly found myself in the midst of a clique: one that even included girls and women, one of whom, to my great surprise, soon expressed what appeared to be a carnal interest in me.

Unlike anytime in my life up to that point, except for the childhood members of my Jansen Avenue group and my trio of high-school lunch stablemates, I was part of a cohesive little group of patients, dining together and conversing with relative ease. Participating each day in that little coterie, I conveniently overlooked the fact that several of the other members were considerably more sick, mentally, than I was. In a word, rather than suffering from psychoneuroses like anxiety and panic, they were full-fledged psychotics. To be blunt, crazy. Many had been committed involuntarily, and constantly sought ways to get out of what they perceived as a veritable prison. I, on the other hand, felt safer than I had in a long time, and had no desire to leave.

Maintaining daily relations with a group of seriously ill people wouldn't have been that much of a problem, if it had stopped when I finally was released back to the outside world. By then, a couple of those people had become what I considered to be my only true friends. Furthermore, I'd eased into a romantic relationship with that older female patient – who happened to be married and a mother. Our tryst blossomed after she escaped from the Institute and I was permitted to leave regularly, ostensibly to look for a job. After my release, I kept seeing her sporadically, until we split after a ferocious argument one night.

I kept seeing another former patient longer, but solely as a friend, not a lover. That relationship screeched to a halt when her inherent psychotic behavior reached a crescendo, and she began to accuse me of bizarre transgressions, utterly without foundation. Because we shared a psychiatrist, I had to put a stop to her erratic and unfounded allegations, which demanded a total separation.

A couple of years later, my anxiety and panic symptoms returned full-force, and I signed up for milieu therapy at another psychiatric institution: four all-day sessions each week, incorporating group and individual therapy. Once again, in the context of a mental hospital where the rules of behavior were different, I managed to make a few friends – still a near-impossible task in the outside world – and was part of an impromptu social group. And once again, a woman I took up with in a romantic sense turned absurdly paranoid, unleashing a string of horrific accusations.

Meanwhile, ironically, another woman – also mentally ill but evidently not an angry paranoid – actually demonstrated a keen interest in me as other than a mere friend. Did I drop the crazy lady and turn my attention to the saner one, who was also more appealing sexually? Of course not. Something within me – an inner saboteur – inevitably would propel me toward the worse possible choice in friends or paramours, bypassing any who happened to be comparatively sane and sensible.

While in any institutional setting for the mentally troubled, subtle danger lurks at every step. You begin to feel that you're *defined* as mentally ill – that it's your most prominent attribute by far. As a result, it's tempting to move further and further apart from the conventional world of mundane neuroses. Even after release, there's often a compelling need to cling to some of those "crazy" friends you'd made during a difficult period in your life. It's rarely a wise choice.

Shyness and discomfort with people do have a way of easing with the passage of time. While working independently for decades didn't help, becoming an automotive journalist in the 1980s did. Rather than continuing to work alone, I suddenly found myself to be part of a group: a hundred or so media people who gathered together, usually at the invitation of auto-company executives, to test-drive the latest models at locales all over North America. Amazingly, I seemed to belong to the cocktail-party circuit, attending receptions and dinners which, in the past, would have inspired nothing other than dread of the prospect of having to talk with people.

After marrying shortly before my 36th birthday, friends did ease into my life; but they were mainly people we'd met as a couple. Not until I began traveling regularly as an automotive journalist, in my fifties, did my count of acquaintances – and even a couple of actual friends – start to shoot upward.

Amazingly, a lot of people nowadays attend what are called Meetups: arranged gatherings where people come to meet others with similar tastes or interests. More astounding yet, they seem to look forward to these open-ended meetings with strangers, rather than perceive them as a painful ordeal. Even I belong to one Meetup group, which has monthly meetings, but it's strictly for business purposes: a gathering of eBay sellers.

Looking back now as a senior citizen, except in childhood, I never had a life that incorporated buddies or pals. No gang; no really close group. Oh, it may have appeared to be one at times, but eventually it became evident that most of those folks who were perceived as friends fell short, by any definition of the term.

As expected, the inability to make friends with at least some degree of ease made dating a virtual impossibility during most of my youth. By the time I became a bit more at ease with strangers, I was middle-aged and married; so dating wasn't in the cards then, either.

Fidelity within marriage, incidentally, is nothing to boast about when you've faced no temptations, or observed no opportunities for dalliance. During my 40-year marriage, no woman ever expressed an interest in me beyond ordinary friendship. So, fidelity was never a choice; it was an inescapable requirement.

Now and then, there have been exceptions to the demanding task of talking with strangers and trying to make friends, at least temporarily. When staying for a month or more in the Mexican city of San Cristobal de las Casas, in the southern state of Chiapas, I've taken a room at a budget-level bed-and-breakfast that caters mainly to backpackers and wanderers. Nearly all are just passing through, stopping in this city for only a day or two. Maybe it's the knowledge that I'll never see any of these folks again. They're all coming and going regularly. Whatever the reason, I've actually had quite a few enjoyable, even easygoing, chats with some of these trekkers through the Mexican highlands.

Same with my two extended stays in Paris, courtesy of Airbnb. Earlier in life, I could never have imagined myself living with strangers, but my host and hostess managed to bring out a side of myself that I didn't even realize existed. Though far from ebullient or talkative, I spent my evenings conversing with the two of them, separately or apart, and it wasn't frightening or dreadful at all. Too bad this discovery came so late in life – but that's a lot better than never experiencing such ease with new acquaintances at all.

15

Keeping Friends

Most of us get surprising e-mails now and then: messages that are utterly unexpected. So it was with the one I received late in 2012, from a woman in Florida.

Presumably, she'd found my name on the Internet. She wanted to know if I'd lived on a certain Chicago street in the 1940s.

As it happened, I had indeed lived on that street. Her father, she explained, had shown her an old photograph of himself as a child, with another youngster, and she'd asked him who that was. "That's my friend Jimmy," he'd told her. And that was definitely me, as I realized when I later saw the photo in question: the two of us standing in his backyard, directly across the street from the apartment building in which I lived. The photo had been taken in 1942, according to wording on the back, written by his mother. We were each three years old.

Though I hadn't seen this fellow in some sixty years, my recollections of him were pleasant ones. So I e-mailed him with a few details about my life, and he did likewise.

We later talked once on the phone. At one point, he observed that the two of us had never really done anything together during childhood years. He was right. Yet, we were friends, by virtue of living near the same urban intersection of two side streets. (Fans of singer Jennifer Lopez may recall her referring to herself as "Jenny from the block." Working-class urban dwellers knew exactly what Ms. Lopez meant.)

In any case, the action taken by the daughter of my long-lost friend resulted in a pleasing and utterly unfamiliar feeling of reverie, on my part.

Ordinarily, I haven't a spark of interest in using Facebook,

Google, etc. to try and locate friends or acquaintances from the past. Many of us wonder whatever happened to so-and-so from high school, from the old neighborhood, from our first job, or whatever. I am not among them.

The one time someone from my own past found me decades later, it turned into a debacle. Finally, I remembered that this particular fellow had been a jerk when we were teenagers. So, why should I be surprised when I realized that he still was.

If making friends is a battle for those of us who have trouble with small talk and easy conversation, keeping them isn't a whole lot easier.

I've always had few friends, especially in adulthood. Quite a few acquaintances, but nearly all of them stem from my work during the past 15 or 20 years. Before that, not many acquaintances were part of my life, either.

Except for a couple of friends my wife and I share, no one calls me on the phone just to talk. They never did, at least not since childhood. Not that I called friends in the past very often, either. Personal communication by phone never seemed that essential. Or, perhaps that's just how I rationalized it, while inwardly seething about being rejected in that way.

Maybe that's why I lack a cell phone, and don't much care if I have a telephone of any kind. Who would I call if I had one? Who'd call me? Ultimately, maybe I'm the one most at fault for a largely friend-free life.

Being aware of my loner status in adolescence and young adulthood, all too often I initiated relationships with the wrong people. Or worse yet, with some who wound up causing harm. Even if it never reached that level, they gave little sign of caring about me and, in my estimation, put up with me only reluctantly, for a while. But when you're desperate to establish a friendship now and then, it's hard not to lower your standards and take up with undesirables – simply because they're there.

Upon closer evaluation, more than one of the people I considered to be a friend in the distant past, or even over a period of decades, never ranked as a real friend at all. Not if we define a friendship as a matter of equivalency, with each person interested in the thoughts, opinions, and activities of the other. Those pseudo-friends, it turned out, were interested solely, or at least mainly, in themselves. They may have done no real harm by indulging in pretend friendship; but when viewed objectively, neither did they add anything pleasurable or rewarding to my life. Nor I to theirs, I must admit.

Of course, not all quasi-friendships are benign. Some are harmful indeed. In one episode of HBO's *Girls*, the inspired and uniquely observant slice of 20-something urban life created by Lena Dunham, her character – Hannah Horvath – refers to the dilemma of having "bad friends." Fortunate folks who've been blessed with *good* friends, or at least passable friends, might have trouble grasping that concept. Those of us who've been taken advantage of, or used by, people we'd thought were friends, likely nodded in agreement upon hearing that term.

Note that a truly "bad" friend is not nearly the same as a person who simply isn't, and never was, a particularly good friend. Or perhaps, didn't qualify as a friend at all, even if your relationship was long-standing.

No, the baddies are the ones who manage to get you in trouble: taking advantage of some weakness or insecurity in your personality to induce you to do something that goes against your principles. Or is just plain wrong, if not blatantly immoral or illegal.

In my own past life, one of those undesirables heads the list handily. When the two of us were driving around aimlessly one night, long ago, he proposed an action that clearly qualified as just plain wrong, by even the most flexible measure. Though I had no interest in what he proposed, he was insistent and forceful, whereas I was weak and gullible. Also, as usual in those days, seriously intoxicated.

Having been acquainted with me since high school, he knew exactly which buttons to push to induce me to go along: mainly, the fact that I had trouble saying "no" to someone I considered a friend. As a result, I've spent every day of my subsequent life regretting that incident; while I have no doubt that he has little or no recollection, or maybe even forgot all about it by the next day. Bad friends are particularly adept at getting *you* to take the blame for their misdeeds.

Not that I blame this fellow entirely. It wasn't his fault that I was so weak that I couldn't resist his pressure to participate in a misdeed.

Having few friends definitely makes you value the existence of those who *do* fill your life. And to lament their loss when they slip away.

They do, too. Sadly, too many people have disappointed me over the years, and ceased to be friends – or even acquaintances. Some have displayed a lack of ethics that I could not abide. Some became overly self-absorbed, and cavalier about maintaining a friendship. Others turned greedy or changed their basic views of life. A few demonstrated an overblown opinion of their place in the world, which I found to be tacky and tiresome.

Eventually, I've walked away from each of those relationships, even though I knew that meant my already meager stock of friends would decline by yet one more. Without question, shortage of friends is mostly my own fault, for being overly judgmental and expecting too much of people.

What, exactly, *is* a friend, anyway? Lots of definitions come to mind. Someone who's always ready to help, perhaps, without demanding an explanation or expecting anything in return. Or, one who is willing to advise, or accept your advice, but only if that counsel is wanted. Friends can certainly criticize each other when appropriate, and even vie against each other at times; but they don't engage in one-upmanship or petty jealousies.

Certainly, a friend is someone you like to be around; and presumably, the reverse. We feel comfortable letting friends know certain details – even secrets – about ourselves. Unless we know something about each other, we can't truly be friends; but that doesn't mean we have to know *everything*.

If we define a friend as someone you can depend on, and

confide in, my total shrinks further yet. Currently, I can count the number of true friends on part of one hand, and that total includes my wife.

All too often – likely out of desperation – I wound up almost forcing myself upon people I'd recently met, presumably hoping they would become actual friends. Looking back, I can hardly believe how overly intense I could be in those days.
This happened when I joined the Studebaker Drivers Club, a group of car enthusiasts who were particularly fond of the automobiles built by that Indiana company, which expired in 1966. Although I began as a courteous and cordial member of that organization, active in producing its monthly newsletter, I soon evolved into what can only be termed a pest.
Once I'd established an acquaintance with someone who didn't seem to want to avoid me, I might start turning up at his or her door, even at odd times. I'd become clingy, to use a word that wasn't heard in those days but has gained currency of late as a vivid descriptor of a certain personality trait. This could happen even with arms-length acquaintances, as I felt impelled to take advantage of the fact that we'd established some sort of relationship, yet fearful that it would soon evaporate.
Which it would, largely because I tried too hard and pushed too forcibly, trying to fire up a friendship that wasn't destined to make it past the first spark. If any past members of that Studebaker club happen to read this chapter, please accept my apology for behaving so boldly back then. It was an act of self-desperation on my part.

Sure, I envy people with multiple good friends. Who wouldn't? When one of my colleagues told me about his brother, who's been his best friend throughout their long lives, I felt left out.
Quantity of friends isn't everything, of course. Far better to have one good friend than a dozen who fall short on the basic requirements of true friendship.
Not until late in life did I realize that several people whom I'd considered to be friends over the years, sometimes for decades, had

really been more like unusually long-term acquaintances. Makes me all the more appreciative of the tiny handful that do remain, led by my long-suffering wife: my best friend by far.

16

Dancing

This chapter shouldn't even be here. By all logic, I should have learned how to dance in the gymnasium at James G. Blaine grammar school in Chicago, while in seventh (or was it eighth?) grade.

Oh, they tried. Can't blame the teacher at all for my lack of prowess. But when you're dealing with a wimpy kid who's petrified of being in the same room with a gaggle of girls, much less expected to lay a finger upon one of them, the challenge rises to a crescendo.

Mere moments before Lesson One was underway, I demonstrated how difficult this class was going to be. Before any lesson began, boys were told to pick a partner and get ready to practice and learn. Since the mix was just about evenly split between boys and girls, this shouldn't have been a problem. But again, they didn't know who they were dealing with when that request was issued.

Within seconds, every boy in the gym had walked up to a girl and asked her to join him. Every boy except me. At that point, only two girls were left. One was a buxom 15-year-old, practically an adult compared to me, a barely-12-year-old twerp. The other was the girl who lived upstairs from me. A year or two earlier, as described in Chapter 13, she had been my first date. We'd gone together to the local theater to watch *The Treasure of the Sierra Madre*, the 1948 film version of the classic adventure tale of gold prospectors in Mexico, by B. Traven.

Afterward, when the neighborhood boys got wind of our romantic escapade at the Music Box Theater, the taunts began. Unwilling or unable to stand up and be counted as a young man attracted to women, I sheepishly retreated, and eased up on my friendship with my upstairs neighbor. How could I admit to my 10-year-old male friends that I actually *liked* her? Liked a girl!

(Years later on-screen, a somewhat older Tony Manero, as portrayed by John Travolta in *Saturday Night Fever*, was asked a similar question by his dancing partner: could he merely be friends "with a *girl*?")

Back in 1950, my young neighbor stood next to this older female person, each waiting to see who I would choose as my very first partner in the new realm of ballroom dancing. I'm surprised that I'm not still on that gymnasium floor, trying to decide between the two.

Finally, still wary of attracting comments from the guys on the block, I opted for the older girl. Placing my hand gently upon her back, I could feel the back strap of her sizable brassiere. No matter how hard I tried not to think about it, her exuberantly abundant breasts protruded toward my chest, almost threatening to make contact, despite the arms-length stance that was mandatory during dance class.

Is it any wonder that the box steps we were instructed to practice failed to result in even the slightest semblance of grace or dignity? Instead, I clomped around, going through the motions of creating an invisible rectangle on the gym floor, my feet hitting the slatted wood like lead weights dropped from high above. Two left feet? It was as if both of mine had been fitted with heavy boots.

My neighbor, meanwhile, stood on the sidelines, the only girl left behind – a place where I devoutly wished to be myself.

In theory, at least, at Blaine School we learned the steps involved in the Fox Trot, Waltz, even the Charleston (a lively 1920s dance that was already long since passe). But nearly all of them failed to translate to appropriate foot movements.

It's easy to see why. I was petrified during each lesson, so blockage between brain and feet was a virtual certainty.

Also, the idea of laying a hand on a girl, even chastely upon her back, was simply too much to cope with. Not that the idea was unappealing. Quite the opposite. It was *way too* appealing, but totally impeded by an overabundance of fear.

Incompetent

Oddly enough, I do have rhythm. At least, I've always thought so. Listening to certain favorite pop tunes and rock classics, I can hardly refrain from tapping my toes and even swaying my torso – just a trifle, so as not to be noticed, of course. I've even been known to wield pretend drumsticks, and to keep time by working my fingers as if playing the old accordion that I struggled to learn during kidhood. More on that fiasco in Chapter 18.

The trouble lies in translating the rhythm I feel inside, down to my feet. They just don't cooperate, preferring to do little more than shuffle around aimlessly. Or, try to head for the door.

Moreover, they've never been properly trained, and quickly forgot what little they once learned.

Hardest of all, curiously, was the free-form, unscripted dancing that began to replace formal dance steps in the 1960s and beyond. It was the kind of dancing that has no particular steps, where partners stay apart, and which virtually everybody had always seemed able to do – except for me. I never really understood what to do with one's feet while engaged in modern dancing – the kind where partners don't touch at all. Only rarely did I attempt to join in that particular revolution, and typically only when intoxicated.

Many years later, when I wound up dancing with an old friend at her daughter's wedding reception, I was startled to see that she had this kind of impromptu, informal action in mind. I tried. My feet moved somewhere or other, roughly in time to the music. I even managed to sway various portions of my body, in an attempt to mimic actual dancing as practiced by the adept. What I looked like to observers in the room, I cannot begin to imagine. In my own mind, I was doing little more than flailing about. To this day, I've no idea whether I looked simply stupid or slightly adept on that occasion.

Not every one of my attempts at dance steps failed miserably. In a 2012 biography of Leonard Cohen, the great poet/singer notes that he thought the Twist was the best dance of them all in the late 1950s and early 1960s. Curiously, I found myself able to do the

Twist rather well – even enthusiastically. Maybe it was because the feet really had little to do; most of the motion was in the hips.

Yet, I also found myself capable of at least minimal skill in the Cha-Cha and the Polka. At a wedding in the Sixties, for instance, I turned in a passable performance of the latter. Actually, it was a rather vigorous rendition of the Polka, almost leaping (by my sedate standards) around the floor and not even threatening my partner's feet in the process. That was something of a surprise, since weddings usually brought out the worst in my shyness, causing me to sit uncomfortably, largely silently, at a table, for the duration of the seemingly joyful festivities. And of course, to partake of as many alcoholic drinks as possible.

Something about the rhythms involved, and the emphatic nature of the steps, made those two versions workable even to a ballroom incompetent such as myself. Or, maybe it was the simple fact that even though the steps were formalized, unlike slow dancing, there was no need to hold your partner reasonably close. In that sense, they were non-threatening to a person whose discomfort with the opposite sex had not yet eased appreciably.

Once while in college, as we've already observed, my four roommates hosted a party at our off-campus house. At some point during the evening, I found myself wrapped in the arms of a delightful co-ed (that's what they were called in those ancient days), swaying erotically around our living room in a dance that seemed to have no particular form or rules. Too bad that night had to end so badly, with an episode of driving while intoxicated and arrest: Yet another example of disasters that inevitably accompanied any experience that should have been fun.

Watching good dancers has always been enticing, even if my own efforts were nonexistent or awkward. During my later teens, as we've seen in the chapter on Skating, I was particularly envious of the jitterbuggers at the Hub roller rink – a popular hangout for young working-class Chicagoans. I didn't care much about their skill on skates, but several of the most sharply-attired hoods (a Fifties term for hoodlums, and those who tried to look the part) were simply magnetic on the little dance floor out in the lobby, swinging their invariably-hot babes to delectably rhythmic beats.

Though I managed to avoid opportunities to dance through most of my life, now and then I did take the step (so to speak). On my first date with my wife, for instance, we wound up at a large cocktail lounge with a dance floor. Much to my own surprise, I asked her to dance. Can't say our hesitant movements around the floor quite qualified as authentic dancing, but at least that evening counts in my skimpy lifetime scorebook of almost-valiant attempts.

My mother had always been an excellent, and avid, dancer. She met my father at a dance, in Chicago, during the Great Depression. Ballroom dancing was a popular, and inexpensive, pastime in those difficult days.

So, why did I have so much trouble, experiencing all that anguish, with a pastime that millions upon millions of people have *fun* doing? Naturally, the primary reason for my inability, as always, was an unwillingness to let myself be observed doing poorly. That's what turns us into wallflowers.

One of Norman Mailer's many novels was titled *Tough Guys Don't Dance*. Though I'm certainly no tough guy, I do not dance, either. The difference is, I regret my inability to shine at least a little bit on the dance floor.

17

Singing

You know the old assertion, "he couldn't carry a tune in a bucket?" Well, I couldn't even *find* that tuneless bucket, if pressed.

Like most male youngsters, I was a boy soprano until high school – but not the kind you'd want to listen to. Had Luciano Pavarotti heard what oozed past my teeth as music played, he wouldn't have placed his hand on my shoulder in appreciation, as he did to a young boy in a widely-seen concert video of such a duet. No, he probably would have given up opera, repelled by the discordant notes assaulting his discerning ears.

I love opera. Ever since I saw my first operatic performance, *Madame Butterfly*, while in college, I've been a big fan. When I hear a renowned tenor or mezzo-soprano intoning the words of Puccini or Verdi, in particular, I can be driven to tears.

My musical tastes are diverse, though, when it comes to the human voice. As a classical-music lover, I adore the choral portions of Beethoven's Ninth Symphony, for instance. But I'm also overcome by Sarah Brightman and Andrew Bocelli in their duet of *Time To Say Goodbye*; by Queen's *Bohemian Rhapsody*; by The Eagles' *Hotel California*; by Pete Seeger and Joan Baez; by Bob Dylan and Bonnie Raitt.

Unlike many of my fellow senior citizens, I also appreciate what's sung by far younger performers, though I don't keep up with contemporary pop music as much as I used to. Oddly, just about the only pop vocals that fail to do much for me are those that were popular in the Fifties, when I was a teenager.

As long as I don't have to try and sing myself, the human voice is a marvel indeed. Thankfully, few people have ever heard me make an attempt.

Incompetent

My vocal range invariably seemed to straddle two adjacent realms, cutting off the high end of one and the low end of the other. Trying to sing solo is the worst, but doing so in unison isn't much better. After muttering a few initial words in something resembling song, I'd simply stop and turn to mouthing the lyrics. Or sometimes, not even that. Whether in song or in regular voice, I'm stymied by the need for cooperative, joint efforts, having never been much of a team player.

Back in grade school, everyone had to be in the chorus, at least for a while. Most kids were encouraged to belt out the song of the day, to the best of their ability. The discordant voices among us were *discouraged*, at least subtly and implicitly, from doing so. Who can blame those music teachers? Why would they want to hear those lush musical notes turned into mush by a youthful singer who couldn't emit a pleasing sound if his or her life depended on it.

No, not even in the shower am I able to sing. I wouldn't want to subject *myself* to those repellent tones I would produce, any more than I'd want to make *you* hear them.

As it happens, my wife is another non-singer, but one who likes to try to vocalize now and then, despite difficulty getting quite into tune. It's one of many ways in which our childhoods, which took place in cities 150 miles apart, were amazingly similar – even though we first met far later in life.

Surprisingly, I can read music, at least to a small degree. But tying an actual sound emanating from one's mouth (or a musical instrument) to one of those notes is a skill beyond my comprehension.

18

Music

If there's one skill that I'd like to have been able to acquire, more than anything else in life, it would be playing a musical instrument. It's second only to the inability to learn a language thoroughly, as something I regret dearly.

In elementary school, music lessons were available – but with practical limitations. I really wanted to learn the piano, but few working-class Chicagoans had pianos at home, and the class had just one. How was that logistical blip handled? We were each given a lifesize cardboard cutout of a piano keyboard. Part of one, anyway, as the cardboard wasn't long enough to encompass all of the instrument's keys.

Strangely, the impact of tapping away on a strip of cardboard failed to inspire much in the way of musical attainment or pleasure.

So, what did I wind up playing? Or more accurately, trying – but failing – to play? The accordion. Yes, my family managed to buy me one of those then-familiar instruments, which were already viewed in the 1940s and 1950s as relics of the past. It was a secondhand accordion, a basic model with few frills. Not that it mattered. It could have been the most gadget-riddled accordion on the planet, and I wouldn't have learned to play it any better than I did.

Despite a string of lessons by a dedicated private instructor, all I could manage was to play the keys by rote, rigorously following the printed musical score. Passion? Feeling? Joy of creating sound? Not a bit of it. My playing was stiff, mathematical, robotlike, devoid of any feeling – as if marching somberly in unison, while made of wood.

Recitals were part of the learning process, and I dreaded the day when mine was due. I *knew* how bad I was. Nothing could change that fact. Why, then, should I humiliate myself by appearing onstage and pretending I had a shred of ability? To this day, I can't imagine how awful I sounded, especially when playing a duet with a young fellow who actually knew how to get something worthwhile out of the instrument. It was not my finest hour.

Not that accordion players were all nerds and geeks living in the past. Some were actually quite good. A middle-aged friend of my father's even took to composing music herself, rather than rely on the scores that were available in print. My father took exception to her efforts. In his world, someone from the working class trying to achieve anything of a cultural nature was being uppity, attempting to become someone they were not.

In my early twenties, though, I met a young woman who was a rather accomplished flute player, and had decided to take up the accordion. Needless to say, she made that instrument sing, even when she was still in the learning stage. She even looked great while pulling and pushing the two sides of the accordion, extending and then diminishing the bellows-filled gap between them. No surprise, though. In addition to being a talented musician, she was a former beauty queen, having come close to being named Miss Chicago not long before.

Like most of us who are devoid of musical ability, I had friends who'd become expert players. One of my best friends in childhood spent a good chunk of each day at the piano, practicing, and it was well worth the effort. By the time he was in his teens, he could manipulate those piano keys in ways that I couldn't even imagine, whether playing classics or be-bop.

At the other end of the spectrum, another friend during my grade school days spent considerable hours trying to learn the violin. His efforts did not result in a musical career, nor in more than the mildest demonstration of expertise. I understood fully.

Now and then during my twenties, someone would try to teach me the rudiments of some instrument – especially the guitar, which was becoming so popular in the 1960s. One of those impromptu instructors lived upstairs in my building – one of the many furnished rooms I resided in during my late teens and twenties. I'd watch his fingers on the frets, and hear the satisfying result as he strummed the strings. When I tried to duplicate his finger positioning, all I could think of was that my fingers were way too big to hold down those little strings. In reality, my fingers were average in thickness, or perhaps even a little smaller. Clearly, I was missing some basic principle of guitar-playing. I still can't understand how anyone can get their fingers right where they should be, much less move them around the guitar neck at dizzying speeds.

A few years later, I actually bought myself a guitar, hoping to try and teach myself. Even before opening the box, I knew it was a huge mistake, and returned the guitar to the store. Far better that it would wind up in the hands of someone who was able to make good use of it, I figured. In my possession, it would simply join the sad stack of prior acquisitions that I'd never touch again.

Amazing as it was to watch people play an instrument well by reading music, what absolutely floored me were those who could "play by ear." One day, a college roommate sat down at the piano in the living room of our rented house and just started playing. Loud. Emphatically. Correctly. All I can say about that episode, even today, is that it demonstrated that all of us have potential within our minds that will never be employed – but that some of us, somehow, manage to release one or two of those innate capabilities.

Ironically, I always wanted to be a musician. Better say that again: Yes, despite my utter and total lack of elemental talent or skill, I could foresee a life as a professional musician. That's not quite as idiotic as it sounds. What I liked about that life was the milieu in which many folk, rock, jazz and pop musicians worked: dark, smoky bars and clubs, presumably populated by shady characters and willing women. That sort of occupational life oozed a certain notoriety that was hard to resist.

It's probably a good thing that I didn't have even the tiniest amount of talent, because I'd have spent my life in a web of frustration and rejection in that cutthroat business. Totally devoid of talent, I couldn't delude myself into thinking there could ever be a possibility of turning into a musician, no matter what I did or how hard I tried. That was sheer lunacy.

It's a bit like my infatuation with the life of the fashion photographer played by David Hemmings in the 1966 British film, *Blow-Up*. Naturally, I knew I had no talent for photography or any of the arts, so I realized I could never be part of that life. Still, watching him pilot his Rolls-Royce convertible around London, attracting the attentions of a stream of nubile young lovelies and elegantly mature beauties, generated a certain elemental appeal. So, I contented myself with wearing white Levi's, similar to the attire sported in every scene by Hemmings' photographer.

Sadly, I cannot leave this chapter without recounting one of my frightfully embarrassing episodes of pretending to lead a band, or an orchestra. Now, plenty of people have enjoyed this sort of fantasy. But this was during my drinking days. In my advanced state of inebriation, I stood in front of a big picture window in the home of my cousin in California, where I was living temporarily while searching for a job. All the neighbors could see this drunken fool, furiously going through all the motions with what may have looked like passion, but was really sheer stupidity.

19

Art and Drawing

No one ever expected any of the youngsters at James G. Blaine elementary school and Lane Tech High to turn into artists. This was working-class Chicago, after all. Artists belonged to some other realm, some other area of society. Maybe some other, little-known species. No, all we were expected to do was learn to make a few drawings that roughly resembled – well, something.

If I had any hope for turning artwork into a pastime, if not an occupation, that hope was dashed by my fifth grade teacher. Rather than simply say I had no ability in the art department, early on she latched onto the fact that I was left-handed. This was the late 1940s, and vestiges of antique attitudes toward the unconventional could still be found. She was convinced – and made sure I understood – that my left-handedness was the cause not only of my deficiencies in the creation of art, but had turned me into an introvert.

She even wanted to convert me to right-handedness. And would have, had my father not come to school to intervene. This was quite a surprise. Like most urban working men of that era, he ordinarily had little to no interest in my schoolwork, or what was happening in class. To have him show up at school to object to a forcible change of handedness came awfully close to a miracle.

Of course, some of those fifth-graders could produce nearly adult-like work. I could barely manage stick figures. So, while the teacher was wrong about causes, her appraisal of my meager talent was right on the mark. Nobody expects grade-schoolers to turn out great works of art, but they're at least expected to grasp the basics.

All through school, too, I had friends who were actual artists. Some were trained, others not; but all exhibited talent well beyond their years. On the other hand, some of those friends and acquaintances *thought* they were capable artists, perhaps destined for greatness; but the cold, hard world of reality soon dispensed a rather different evaluation.

Once I got to high school, a passel of artistic success – albeit different in form – came my way, much to my surprise. Because this was a technical high school, every boy (no girls allowed in those days) had to take four semesters of drafting – also known as mechanical drawing.

In view of my utter lack of artistic skill, amplified by that fifth-grade teacher but also obvious to anyone who'd observed my efforts, I never expected to excel at any sort of artistic or semi-artistic endeavor. Yet, drafting was different: essentially all lines, angles, squares, circles. In other words, mathematical – and that was what I was good at. Numbers come easily to me. Far more so than shapes and colors.

Even architectural drawing turned into a pleasant pastime, at which I could exhibit at least an elementary level of skill. That was kind of fun, preparing meticulous, accurately-rendered images of a home or building in several views, making use of angles, perspective, and rather intricate detail work. This sort of thing, I was almost adept at. Why, I even earned good grades as a budding draftsman.

The only complaint that instructor had about my work was that it was likely to be smudged, due to improper erasure technique. Neatness was never my primary virtue. Some might even have called me messy. Still, apart from a bit of imperfection in the cleanliness department, my finished "plates" represented one of the few examples of any sort of artistic skill that I would ever experience.

Those skills actually remained useful later in life, unlike most things we learn in high school. When writing how-to books and articles on technical subjects in the 1970s and early 1980s, I was able to create passable mechanical-type line drawings to accompany my text.

But "real" art and drawing? Not a chance. Glance at a drawing I once did of a person's hand, for example, to illustrate a certain process for fixing an automobile engine. That detached hand looked like something that might come thrusting out at you in a trashy 3-D horror movie, disfigured and inhuman.

20

Games

It was a friendly poker game, at a longtime friend's apartment. Only rarely had I ever played poker in a group, even though I had a pretty good grasp of the game's rules and statistical elements. Playing against real people added a dimension that in my case detracted from, rather than added to, the pleasures of poker.

At one point in the evening, for a change, I believed I had a winning hand. So, I put my five cards down on the table, face up, waiting to gather my winnings. The others looked a bit confused, but I dragged in the coins and bills. Only afterward did I realize that I may have shown my hand *before* the draw rather than afterwards – a mistake that even the rankest beginner would never, ever make.

That's my level of poker-playing, and the way I've participated in games all my life. Not only do I never win, but I'm likely to make the grossest, most embarrassing errors.

Trouble is, I don't much *care* if I win. Certainly, not enough to struggle. Mainly, I just lack any sort of competitive instinct, whether in sports, games, business, or anything else.

Simply put, there's never been a game I was good at, or even played at an adequate beginner level.

I'd grown up in a household where weekly poker games, fueled by alcohol and tobacco smoke, were on the regular schedule. Not that I played, of course; that game, played for money, was for grownups. I just watched (when permitted) and listened.

Worst of all are games where your opponent(s) can see what you do, and what you're contemplating. Chess, of course, is the most troubling in that respect. Facing a chessboard, you're fully aware of your opponent's moves. That part might be okay, except it means your opponent also is aware of *your* moves. Or, your near-paralysis of mind, sitting there trying to decide what move to make with that enemy agent's gaze bearing down upon the board.

Draw Poker is more like it. Conceal your hand, at least until you win (if ever, in the case of incompetents). But that doesn't eliminate the dread of interaction with other players. In Poker, as in nearly all games, it's intimidating and worrisome. Most definitely, not fun. No wonder, then, that on the rare occasions when I do elect to play poker, it's at an electronic machine, whether in Las Vegas or at a local casino.

I can almost appreciate the professional poker players who wear sunglasses and hoodies, to help conceal their contemplation. Still, it does seem a bit like cheating, since "reading" the other players' faces has long been an integral part of serious poker.

Not that I cared very much about games, with one prominent exception. For years, I wanted to become a passable pool player, if nothing else. Not an expert, able to "run the table" with ease. Nothing remotely like Fast Eddie Felsen, as portrayed by Paul Newman in the 1962 film that's long been among my favorites, *The Hustler*. Just someone who might possibly be victorious once in a great while. Didn't seem that much to ask, or expect. But as always, reality intervened.

Much of my early twenties was spent in a bar/bowling alley with a pool table, playing with a particular friend. Having learned the game while in the peacetime military, he became a top-notch player, often able to win money using his skills. I, on the other hand, despite long hours at the table, never progressed even to the beginner stage.

As best I can recall, I never won a game. Ever. Even when playing against first-timers who could barely hold the cue stick in a proper manner.

My regular opponent would suggest the right amount of "English" to apply to the next shot, so the cue ball would wind up in prime position. Wasted advice. I was lucky to hit the object ball at all, so whether I made contact high or low, to the left or the right, mattered not a whit. My shots were invariably just a little off, no matter how carefully I prepared and how intently I studied all the angles. Whether that quirk was due to faulty eyesight (being strongly near-sighted since childhood), nervousness, trying too hard, simple lack of talent, or all of the above, I'll never know. But I'll always wonder.

Tossing coins was another youthful endeavor that yielded incessant failure. Most of my efforts were against this same friend with whom I shared a pool table. No matter how close my coin came to the winning line, his measured nearer yet. Usually, *a lot* nearer. Playing double or nothing one day, I believe my debt to him after a string of unbroken losses reached into the tens of thousands of dollars. Maybe millions. Fortunately, he never tried to collect.

Some games I simply avoided. Checkers always seemed too simple; chess, too complex and cerebral. Blackjack was too fast. My first attempt at blackjack, sitting at a professional table, was in Reno. The minimum bet was two dollars, and I had a ten-spot at hand to wager. Within what seemed like seconds, it was gone. The whole ten. Reluctantly stepping away from the table, I had virtually no recollection of the whirlwind of cards that had come and gone during those seconds. And my wallet was ten dollars lighter.

Underneath, of course, lies a deep perception of myself as a loser. If you've never won at anything, never even come close, what other outcome could there be?

My father – an avid sports and game player – was unquestionably a winner, in his own mind and to a large extent in reality. Most everyone else I knew leaned in that direction, too, when it came to games and athletic contests. They might not win every time, but often enough so the concept of victory had to be lodged in their brains.

Practice makes perfect. We all learned that from an early age. Well, in my case, that old adage never worked at all. For us incompetents, our prowess inevitably takes a *downward* slide with practice.

All too often, my first attempt at a new game turned out to be my best, and it was downhill from there. First time I bowled, for example, I got a 93. Real bowlers would call that meager or worse, but I believe it was also my *best* score ever. Subsequent sessions at the bowling alley yielded even punier totals.

Something in my brain just doesn't accept the concept of games and game-playing. Maybe it's my almost total lack of competitive spirit. Never have I been able to muster anything approaching the kind of must-win mentality that's evident in nearly everyone around me, and practically everyone I encounter.

Clearly, most people want to play, and most of them want to win, no matter what the game may be. "Frankly, my dear," as Clark Gable advised Vivien Leigh (as Scarlett O'Hara) in *Gone With the Wind*, "I don't give a damn."

Now and then, however, I've managed to demonstrate a modest twinge of skill – at least during childhood. If memory serves, I was one of the acceptable players at the game of Ledge. Younger and less-urban readers may not know that Ledge was a street game played by apartment dwellers. Why? Because it consisted of throwing a rubber ball against a brick apartment-building wall, hard, aiming for the stone ledge that protruded right at the base of the brick surface. Scoring was similar to baseball. Hit the ledge right, at the sharp edge, and the ball bounced energetically back into the street, where your opponents were waiting to try and catch it. Strike that ledge with true precision, and the ball could sail over their heads, for a Home Run. Miss the ledge, even by a hair, and it wobbled feebly into the adjacent grass.

Only when the games – and the sports – turned serious and well-organized did my early prowess evaporate.

As for non-athletic games, one of the few I ever enjoyed, and could play effectively, was called London Taxi: a board game that my wife and I played while visiting her relatives in England. Another game played in London yielded quite a few laughs. That one involved tossing tiny, miniature pigs, trying to make each of them land upright. As the instructions pointed out, if one pig happened to land atop another, that was simply *uncivilized*. No wonder I enjoyed those tiny piggies.

21

Languages

Of all my regrets in life, one of the greatest is my inability to become at least mildly proficient with one foreign language: namely, Spanish. Latin-American Spanish, in particular. After a lifetime of Spanish learning (allegedly), my proficiency with the language barely reaches the level of mediocrity. How anyone could bring home so many Spanish tapes, DVDs, CDs, books and pamphlets from the library over the years, yet fail to master the language enough to converse comfortably with a child, is shameful.

Of course, it's well known that inability to learn foreign languages is a common failing among Americans. If so, are we simply stupider than people from Europe, Asia, Africa, or elsewhere in the Americas? Is there some bizarre gene within us that makes us immune to understanding languages other than the one with which we began life?

My Spanish studies began in high school, long, long ago. For two years (four semesters) I faithfully studied the vocabulary and grammar, even earning good grades in the process. Later in life, I began traveling to Mexico periodically, including several multi-month stays. None of it made a particle of difference in overcoming my resistance to gaining a real, effective acquaintanceship with Latin-American Spanish.

Not having a working knowledge of the language after decades of sporadic study is an absurdity of epic proportions. Shameful as it is to admit, I've been studying for more than half a century, yet cannot carry on a simple conversation with a Spanish-speaking person, or understand more than snatches of dialogue in a Spanish-language movie.

How is that possible? How could anyone be so dense, so unable over a period of decades to absorb enough of a language to converse at the level of a youngster?

Oh, I can manage when I'm in Mexico. I'll never be unable to ask directions, order a meal, find the bus station, and so on. But converse with a Mexican? Even on the most elementary level? Never happened.

All I can do is recall with dread attending a performance in the Mexican town in which I was living in the 1970s, and being introduced by Manuel, my Spanish instructor, to a gentleman sitting behind me. This new acquaintance then unleashed a torrent of Spanish, for what seemed like an eternity. Despite all my classes and independent study up to that time, I understood not a word. Nothing. *Nada*. My brain was vacant. All I could say at the end was *Buenas noches* (good evening). Now, what could be more embarrassing than that?

On the other hand, three decades later I was back in the same town, taking one-on-one lessons with a native woman who spoke virtually no English. Half of each class focused on grammar, but the second half involved talking about anything: politics, local economics, cultural events in the area, movies and books. It was strictly Spanish. Not a word of English was uttered by either of us, yet we understood each other quite well. Now, why couldn't I translate that experience and attitude into contact with people on the street, or in a café?

Nothing mysterious about it, really. It's as if I have an inner saboteur in my head, always ready to stop me from taking positive steps to enhance my ability with the language. Or with much of anything else in life; the saboteur is quite versatile.

As I write this chapter, I'm in Paris for the sixth time, yet again embarrassed and ashamed to admit how little French I've permitted myself to learn. It's as if I prefer to be humiliated every time I stop into a café or need to buy a railroad ticket.

Unlike most of my instances of incompetence, this one has a tangible cause – and it's one that's familiar to a good many folks who've tried and tried to learn languages, and failed repeatedly. We're afraid to let ourselves be heard, to make mistakes or sound stupid. If only we could relax a little and let those foreign words ease their way out, maybe one day we'd be able to say, out loud, without holding back: "*Yo hablo español bien.*" Or, "*je parle très bien français.*" Tragically, six decades after those first high-school Spanish classes, I still can't say I speak adequately, much less well.

22

Completing Tasks

Maybe it's just plain laziness. Or stubbornness. Obstinacy, perhaps? Whatever the cause, it's a rare day when I actually complete anything I've started.

My "things to do" and "things to finish" list reaches back not just for days, nor for weeks, but for months. I mean, some items on that list have been there for years already, with no completion date in sight.

A college roommate once referred to himself as an active member of the "half-a-book club," noting that he seldom managed to read a book all the way through. Well, I've scored a lifetime of unfinished, half-done (or barely-started) projects. Half a book? I'm more apt to set those books aside after meandering through no more than a few pages. I always have a stack of library books sitting around the apartment, few (if any) of which will actually be read before being renewed, and then eventually returned. Needless to say, my collection of personal books contains few that have actually been read cover to cover, and plenty that have never even been opened.

Letters go unanswered or unread, at least fully. Parcels remain unopened for weeks. Gifts often go unused, or even unpacked, for months. Gift cards may or may not ever be redeemed. While cleaning my office a while back, I came across several gift cards dating back to the 1990s. Actually, they weren't even cards; these were received long before stores switched to plastic cards, when they still used paper for such purposes.

Unanswered e-mails reach back for months, if not years. Maybe even decades. As I write these words, my laptop's "In Box" contains 5,749 e-mail messages. Plus, all those that I've haphazardly managed to move into save-it folders, typically never to be viewed again. My sole consolation is when I hear about other computer users whose In Boxes contain tens of thousands.

Those projects that did get finished, such as a few model cars and planes in the distant past, looked like they'd been assembled and detailed by a distracted six-year-old wearing heavy gloves. Maybe blindfolded, too. Not the kind of trophy to proudly display on one's mantel.

One of the many ways in which people are sharply divided is their attitude toward starting and finishing projects – and their actual behavior when the time comes. When you're assigned to a project, do you start right in on it? That's what my wife is likely to do. Or, do you take a quick glance at the project, then quickly set it aside for an amorphous "later?" Naturally, that's my preferred method.

Do you consider the deadline, compared with the volume of what needs to be done? Then, set up a schedule – whether formal or informal – to spread the work through the entire period? Or, does the project continue to sit in that ever-growing "things to do" pile, getting attention only when it happens to be noticed. If then.

Finally, as the deadline draws near, are you likely to be in a relaxed state, because you're confident that it will be completed on time? Or, do you anticipate a frantic, harried push at the last minute. Worse yet, are you one of our group of profound procrastinators, who typically don't even *begin* work on a project until the deadline is already looming.

Ever since early school days, I've been a ranking member of the procrastination-forever contingent. Whether it's been schoolwork, editorial assignments, work projects of any kind, or tasks around the house, I can be counted on to start late and finish – at best – at the very last minute.

As a result, life becomes a series of promises made and promises broken – to oneself as well as to others.

Why do some of us have such trouble finishing anything, while others aren't content until a project is completed, and work intently toward that goal? For one thing, I've always been bored easily. I get tired of projects after only a short while, and am ready to move on to something else. Or, better yet, to enjoy a long rest in my easy chair.

Unrealistic expectations play a role, too. Studies have shown quite conclusively that professional procrastinators can't seem to learn from experience. Even though our performance record from the past clearly reveals that they cannot possibly finish writing a book in the last month before deadline, complete a woodworking project in a week when previous ones took a month, or complete any other task in a shorter period than ever accomplished before, we ignore that reality and somehow assume that it will be different this time.

Most often, too, my ability to complete a project has not improved with practice. My tenth attempt at a task is rarely likely to be any better than the first. Often worse.

I seem to have a strange aversion to finishing anything at all. If eating a snack, for instance, such as nuts from a container, I'll invariably leave the last few morsels untouched. Just can't bear to take the last step, even of a trivial task.

Why would that be? I think it's hard to finish anything, because then it will be done and out of my life. Far better, in my twisted brain, to have that incomplete task lay there indefinitely, festering away.

23

Being Noticed

It was 1962, and I was working as a copywriter for a publisher of catalogs for the electronics industry. This was my first job as a professional writer of any sort. The fellow at the desk across the aisle from mine practically jumped out of his chair when I spoke, standing slightly to the rear of his chair. "Jesus, where'd you come from!" he yelled, practically accusing me of sneaking up on him.

A few years later, I'd left my job as a caseworker for the Cook County Department of Public Aid, in Chicago, after 14 months. After failing to find a new, more adventurous life in southern California, I'd returned to my hometown. A friend who still worked at Public Aid told me how he'd mentioned to a fellow worker, whom we both knew and whose desk had been close to mine, that I was back in the city. "Oh?" was the response. "Did he leave?"

Some of us creep through life largely unobserved, leaving no mark, just taking up space. Not entirely unknown, of course; but disappearing into the woodwork, stuck at the edge of awareness by others, for a sizable proportion of our daily lives.

Being shy and quiet from childhood onward paved the way to fading into the background. People hardly notice you if they don't hear you. Or even detect your presence. Whether intentionally or without thinking, I've always spoken so softly that people have to strain to hear my words. Most of them don't try very hard.

After all, if you sneak up on people (unintentionally, we'll presume) because you don't want to create a stir, the image you create is of someone who's not really there. How can others notice me when I'm so unassuming, so unsure of myself as a human entity.

Childhood and teenage years, into young adulthood and beyond, were spent sitting in the back. Whether at school or anywhere else, my preference was to hide behind others, so as not to be called on by a teacher, a boss, or anyone – whether I knew the answer to their query or not. Through each day, becoming invisible was the goal.

It wasn't simply a question of not being noticed, and taking steps to overcome that trait. More important, I did not wish to participate. At least, not participate beyond the minimum requirement.

Blending into the background persisted into my early career as a journalist, too, which did not emerge until middle age. Even on those rare occasions when I wished to be noticed, some colleagues and contacts failed to acknowledge my presence, even when I was right next to them.

At one driving program for journalists held in Mexico, for example, I wound up partnering with a fellow I'd never met before. I soon learned that he spent part of each year in that particular region of Mexico. Since I'd spent considerable time in Mexico and loved the country, I thought we had something in common, and stated my interest in Mexican life.

It was as if I hadn't spoken at all. After my initial attempt at conversation about a shared interest, for the duration of our drive together, we exchanged not a word. When my driving partner spoke at all, it was to the company person who happened to be riding along, sitting in the back seat. I was just an appendage attached to the front passenger seat, totally ignored.

Invisibility so easily becomes the norm. That, and feeling like you're two people in a single body. One of them manages to squeeze through most of the obstacles of life – when traveling, for instance – dealing at least passably well with any demanding situation. The other barely feels capable of getting up in the morning or addressing the most ordinary tasks. No wonder it's so tempting to let the more capable one take care of most everything, so the little-noticed version can continue hiding in the shadows.

This dual personality can be beneficial, letting you be noticed (and assisted, if need be) while also remaining essentially invisible.

When traveling, for instance, I've dealt with all sorts of obstacles – especially, those related to inadequate language skills. Rather than stand mute when I didn't know what to do, though, I was almost invariably able to blurt out a question to a foreign stranger, study a map until I figured out what was needed, stand back and observe the situation from an alternate perspective, even. That is, the "inner me" took those tangible steps. The external "me" stood quietly behind the scene, petrified, barely able to breathe, much less utter a query or formulate a possible course of action.

Had that portion of my personality been allowed to take over, I'd still be standing on a train platform in Tokyo, unable to decide which train to board. Or, wandering the streets of Cannes, France, trying to find my way back to my hotel as night drew near. On that occasion, the answer to my inquiry came from a child, who somehow understood my frenzied French.

Today, even my wife complains now and then that I move too quietly around our tiny apartment, practically sneaking up on her. At events of any sort, on the other hand, I like to sit up front. I got used to taking the position in my work as a journalist, trying to get close enough to see and hear as much as possible at conferences and meetings. In that one characteristic, at least, I did manage to change myself. Nowadays, I can barely recall those decades of hiding within other people's shadows.

24

Making Decisions

Most of us prefer postponing decisions. Or better yet, finding a way to evade making them after all. Avoidance is hardly an uncommon trait. Just about everyone does it some of the time.

Then, there are those of us who put off deciding on anything, practically *all* of the time. Whenever it's remotely possibly to do so, we prefer to remain undecided.

As is so often the case, it's a matter of degree. What's a simple matter of periodic procrastination for one person, turns readily into outright incompetence for another.

For the truly incompetent avoiders, having to decide which flavor of chewing gum to buy, or which hotel to stay in during a trip, is an exhausting, formidable task. We know without question that whichever choice we make, buyer's remorse is sure to follow. Often as not, within moments of finalizing that decision. A big case of it, too, regardless of the insignificance of the choice that finally was made.

So, what do we do when a seriously *large* decision absolutely must be made. Several paths come to mind here:

1. Get somebody else to make it. This is almost invariably helpful, easing one's mind so it can deal with more important tasks.

2. If no one volunteers, at least work out the details so someone else gets part of the blame if (that is, when) things go wrong. No, we don't want to actually *blame* anyone else for our failings; that wouldn't be right. Would it? Still, a little suggestion that someone else's action might have played a small role in what went wrong never hurts.

3. Drag out the decision-making process as exhaustively as possible. We have to admire lawyers, for instance, who tend to be

masters at arranging postponements, taking advantage of courtroom rules to request – and be granted – delays of every kind imaginable. If we're truly successful in this quest, we might even drag it out until we're on our deathbed, still refusing to specify a course to be followed.

4. Flip a coin. Ask a kid for his or her opinion; or a stranger. Anything is better than having to come up with a solution ourselves.

And remember, the world might end just before the deadline for your next decision. Do you really want to spend your final moments on earth fretting about the choice you made? Postpone it yet again; then, if the world explodes in the meantime, you're golden.

25

Cooking

Not every instance of incompetence is distressing. My lack of cooking skills, for one, doesn't trouble me in the least.

Like the proverbial non-cook who can't even boil water, my incompetence extends fully into the kitchen. Yet, having a pleasantly fully stomach most of the time, I rarely even think about that inability.

Not that I'm *totally* inept at the culinary arts. I can heat a can of soup, probably without having it boil over. I can use a microwave for simple tasks: reheating a cup of coffee, heating a frozen dinner, and especially, warming up leftovers. I can actually turn out a passable grilled cheese sandwich, even one with a slice of ham nestled within.

(I miss the old Toastite device that my family had when I was a teenager. That innovative gadget made it easy to whip up perfectly round grilled cheese sandwiches, snipping off the bread crust all around and forming a neatly sealed parcel of bread and cheese.)

Many years ago, when I invited two hungry young ladies over to my little furnished apartment for dinner, what did we consume? TV dinners and (thawed) frozen strawberries. That was about the limit of my culinary skills then, and it hasn't gotten much better in the intervening half-century.

Once, while visiting my parents in those days, I managed to prepare a passable spaghetti dinner. Why I decided to undertake such a task – one that has never been repeated – is still a mystery. At least, the spaghetti was edible.

Since age 16, I've been a restaurant person. No complaints there. A home-cooked meal has never meant that much to me, though most people seem to consider it a veritable necessity of life.

Incompetent

Maybe it's because we rarely had a sitdown family dinner while I was growing up. My father seldom came directly home from work at dinnertime. Instead, he'd stop off at one of the local taverns, returning home after a few hours. At that time, he'd expect his dinner to be waiting, fully warm, the moment he walked in, unannounced.

He was strictly a meat-and-potatoes guy when he managed to eat. He liked his meals spicy, too. That was a perpetual arguing point, because my mother had once worked as a housekeeper and cook for a doctor who advocated bland food. She continued to prepare meals without spices, though knowing full well that my father would become enraged by the lack of zest.

My mother couldn't teach me even the rudiments of cooking or any sort of household tasks, of course. Why? Because my father, like many working-class males of his generation, disapproved of boys *ever* doing what might be considered women's work. So, taking out the garbage was about the extent of my household duties and education.

Much later, while living with my wife in Las Vegas for two years, in a downtown residential hotel, our sole item of cookware was a heating coil. That simple device was just right for heating soups, Ramen noodles, and the like. My kind of cookery, in other words. Most of the meals my wife and I enjoyed were supplied by one of the downtown hotel-casinos, all of which offered special prices – especially late at night, when we normally had our dinner. Budget-priced buffets, too, were part of our daily sustenance.

Nowadays, pouring cold cereal into a bowl, then slicing a banana on top, is about the limit of my culinary efforts. Maybe a simple cold sandwich now and then. Both my wife and I are whizzes at reheating restaurant leftovers. Haven't tried to fry an egg in quite a while, but I suspect I've not lost that minuscule bit of skill. I do make coffee – and managed to do so while living for a while in Paris, using a clever old mechanical device called the French Press.

When staying with friends, I can look at a fully-stocked refrigerator and amply-filled cupboards, yet find nothing to eat. I never seem to know what has to be cooked, and what doesn't. Facing a fully-equipped kitchen, in any case, I'd be at a loss as to where to begin.

All I can say is, hooray for restaurants. I like to be waited on, and to have a choice of meals, without participating in any way other than paying the check. I'm sorry, however, to see the old-time cafeterias fade into memory; they were convenient and reasonable, a sensible choice for us kitchen incompetents.

So, what about those high-end restaurants that let the customer cook his or her own steak, or some other do-it-yourself setup? Are you kidding? Pay a hefty price, yet have to prepare the food personally? Not a chance!

Campfire cookery? Outdoor barbecues? Not for me. I wouldn't mind eating what's made outdoors. Not at all. But I don't get all excited about either of those prospects. Except when I'm in another country, where outdoor cafés are the delightful norm, I believe meals are meant to be served indoors, on tables, with diners seated on chairs. Preferably in well-lighted eateries, so I can read my newspaper comfortably.

Despite my lack of interest in meal preparation, I do enjoy excellent food. At the same time, I'm fully content with very modest lunches and dinners.

To some of us, I've realized more than once, the neighborhood restaurants and diners that I've always frequented are rather exotic – perhaps even a touch threatening. Some years ago, I had lunch with a PR colleague, and suggested one of my regular spots. To say he was surprised would understate his reaction. This ordinary eatery, which I frequented regularly, reminded him of his childhood growing up in New York City. But I had the distinct impression that he hadn't set foot in such a place since leaving home, decades earlier.

Foodwise, I couldn't be easier to please. I've eaten octopus and sundry seafoods (some unidentifiable) while sitting at street counters in Mexico City and Veracruz. I've savored venison, buffalo, pheasant, grits, New Orleans muffaletta sandwiches and beignets, Mexican churros, goat cheese, Scottish haggis, curds, multiple variants of sushi, and much more. Almost nothing is on my never-eat-it list – except for a bizarre item that I came across at the breakfast buffet in my hotel while visiting Japan. I'll be most content if I never encounter that particular "delicacy" ever again.

Unlike so many of my colleagues with whom I've dined at four-star (or higher) restaurants in the course of my work as a journalist, I love vegetables, and consider a meal incomplete without them. Often as not, I have to remind waitresses that the menu states that a vegetable is included with what I ordered. Conversely, I've watched quite a few colleagues carefully shovel each and every vegetable to the side of the plate, so as not to tarnish their pristine steak or chop and potatoes.

I don't mind frozen dinners, either. While residing for a month in France during 2013, my hostess and I basically survived on them. And many of my other meals consisted of sandwiches bought from the local *boulangerie* (bakery). I'm not the least bit embarrassed to admit that I also have a fondness for Sausage-Egg McMuffins and for Burger King's Sausage/Egg/Cheese Croissanwiches, though the 'burgers at fast-food establishments are markedly less enticing.

I can survive indefinitely on meals made with a heating coil or a toaster-oven. If a microwave is at hand, all the better. A big array of fancy cookware wouldn't mean a thing to me. I wouldn't have the slightest idea what to do with most of the tools, and little interest in finding out.

When people are away from home for a time, they'll often lament the lack of home cooking while on the road. Not me. I don't miss it a bit. If I go a week, a month, even a year without a home-cooked meal, I'm not bothered at all. If I never have one again, it won't be a tragedy.

Neither would I be distressed if given the same meal two or three days in a row. If I were in prison, I doubt that I'd be among those ready to riot over the food. In fact, I once did have lunch in a penitentiary – the same meal served to inmates, I was told. I thought it was just fine, though my companions on that academic tour (for a penology class) did not concur with my appraisal.

In short, I'm easily satisfied in terms of cuisine, as long as I don't have to participate in its creation.

Oddly, in the past few years we've become big fans of the chef shows on cable TV: *Top Chef, Chopped, Restaurant Impossible*. Chicago chef Rick Bayless' show, *Mexico: One Plate at a Time*, has been a special favorite. Not just for the information on food, but for the scenes inside Mexican markets that punctuate the kitchen activities. I've wandered through a number of those markets myself, during extended stays south of the border.

At a media event a few years back, dinner was at a culinary institute. So we journalists had an opportunity to watch an expert chef in action, up close. Their skills and knowledge, not to mention imagination and creativity, simply defy belief.

I'm fascinated by the skills exhibited on those chef shows, as well as the occasional TV series such as HBO's *Treme*, which featured a subplot built around a fast-rising female chef in New Orleans. Yet, little desire to emulate them emerges from those viewing sessions. What does rise to the surface is the sure knowledge that any judge sampling my culinary creation would likely cringe into a frown of distaste, or perhaps run from the dining room, clutching his or her stomach.

Home cooking wasn't always absent during adulthood. At one point in my married life, my wife and I lived in a rented farmhouse in rural Wisconsin, set on a one-acre plot with space for a garden. Not only did she regularly prepare roast dinners, from-scratch cakes and many other appetizing items, she incorporated vegetables grown in our very own garden. For a lifelong urbanite, this was a mysterious and near-magical experience. After five years at this location, all of this personalized gastronomical endeavor was happily abandoned when we moved on, spending the next few years on the road, in Mexico and the Southwest.

So, a big thumbs-up for tasty food. And a big fat zero for kitchen duties.

26

Cleaning

For some kinds of incompetence, no excuses can be permitted. Inability to clean is one of them. Or, should we be more accurate and forthright here, and call it *unwillingness*.

So, why am I so untidy? Why is my office, my bed, my desk invariably such a mess? How can I be so unfazed by dust, by dirty dishes, by grungy floors created by tracked-in Midwestern snow?

Is it laziness? Obstinacy? In addition to lack of patience and ambiguity (it's so hard to tell when something is actually clean), the cause is probably a combination of perfectionism and sloth. Whatever the root reason may be, it's a matter of ultimately failing to get the job done. In addition, and perhaps most important, there's the overall inability to get started – with cleaning or so many other daily tasks.

Trouble is, I tend not to notice that dirt, dust, grime – or much else in my surroundings. At least, not until it reaches an overpowering state.

Years ago, when I lived in a furnished basement apartment on Chicago's North Side, the dust gathered to a thickness that even I couldn't accept. Did I drag out the cleaning equipment, or run down to the store to buy soaps and mops and brooms? I did not. Instead, I just let it continue to accumulate.

When I finally moved out of that apartment, it looked pretty hideous. Even so, I still couldn't bring myself to take action. So, what happened? One of my cousins, having observed how bad it looked on a visit some time previous, took the time and made the effort to come over and clean up the place for me. A herculean effort it was, too. Why she did it, I still don't know. I mean, she had small children at home and an active life, and owed me nothing. Maybe it's because, like most women, she just couldn't abide the thought of anyone departing from a residence and leaving it in such a state. And she knew a true cleanup was beyond me.

I'm fully repentant now, but I don't think I felt nearly as ashamed back then. Somehow, questions of cleanliness just never seemed to matter in my younger days.

A few years earlier, while in college, I gave up a furnished room in mid-semester, and thought I'd done a reasonably good job of cleaning the place. My landlady disagreed. Loudly and vociferously. Never did get my cleaning deposit back on that one. Nor did I deserve it, I have to admit.

My workplace is always cluttered beyond belief, mainly because of my propensity to throw things on the floor as I finish with them. Or, to put them aside for later, in little piles on the floor or stashed haphazardly on any flat surface. Actually, it doesn't even have to be flat.

Worse yet is my rented outside office (20 minutes from my office at home). That two-room suite isn't as much of a mess as it used to be in the past, but that's only because a pair of floods some time back forced me to go through everything.

During the clean-up process, which took my brother and me weeks to complete, we sent about one-third of my stuff to the dumpster, because of severe water damage. Printed materials were so waterlogged that they stuck together in hard, gooey blocks that must have weighed five or six times what they had before the foot-deep water hit. All of those formerly valued items became unrecognizable. It was nearly impossible to tell what they used to be, now that they'd been transformed into hardened mush, attracting mold.

Painful as it was to lose some of those books, papers and documents, the flood did compel me to get organized.

As a rule, nothing much is actually *dirty* at each location (in my admittedly impaired appraisal of such matters). My spaces are just messy, wholly devoid of neatness. Naturally, I always intend to get down there sometime soon to pick up the loose stuff and straighten everything out. But aside from the occasional strenuous clean-up session, typically short-lived, that just doesn't seem to happen.

My aversion to ironing slips in here, too. Nothing too unusual about that, though I recently met a gentleman who said he *enjoys* ironing shirts, in particular. He says he finds it relaxing – even therapeutic. I'd say he is one troubled fellow.

As it happens, I'm married to a woman who likes everything clean and neat and uncluttered. Needless to say, there's been an occasional dispute in our household on that score.

27

Business

"Buy high, sell low." That's been my lifelong motto when engaging in any sort of business transaction. And that's what I told an acquaintance one day – an immigrant from Europe who was dating a relative of mine.

To say he was speechless would be an understatement; and he didn't ordinarily have any difficulty finding words.

What's that you say? I've got it backwards? No doubt, that acquaintance assumed I was either joking or confused.

Sorry, no: I was neither. I stated it just right, and meant exactly what I said. When it comes to business ventures of any sort, that's how my life has always gone. That little phrase is in fact the story of my financial life.

For the business-minded and entrepreneurial among us, buying at a low price and selling for a higher one is indeed the correct method. That's the one that yields a profit in the end: the essence of capitalism, the one that allows you to make money from whatever you're trying to sell.

My lack of business acumen started early, as a 10-year-old struggling to sell metal nameplates door to door. To the best of my recollection, I sold nary a one. A few years later, having failed to find a real part-time job while in college, I became a salesman for Winfield China – a company that used door-to-door salespeople to push dinnerware sets on young women who were contemplating marriage. After months of feeble effort, I sold one set – to a friend who actually wanted one.

Next business failure was a stint with the *Book of Knowledge*, a second-rate encyclopedia set that was popular at the time. We'd be given leads of likely prospects by our sales manager, then went in pairs to visit the unwary folks – usually young couples with small children.

We weren't "salesmen," of course. We were compelled to represent ourselves as office workers for the company, who were simply trying to "place" the encyclopedias with a few selected families in the area, as a promotional gesture.

After making our rounds each evening, we'd meet back at a coffee shop with the sales manager. Eventually, he got tired of hearing me say, over and over, that I'd sold nothing. Then one day, I made an actual sale – to a couple who wanted the encyclopedias so badly that even my meager sales pitch couldn't dissuade them from signing on the dotted line. Realizing that this was not the route to business success, I departed from that organization immediately afterward, glad that I'd been able to chalk up at least one sale along the way.

Even that teeny success wasn't to be when I tried my hand as a telemarketer – or phone solicitor, as we were called in those days. A longtime friend was in this business at the time, demonstrating true skill at setting up appointments for a home-improvement company. Not a day passed when he didn't manage to acquire at least one solid prospect. During my brief stint on the phones (which I dreaded), my scorecard of appointments made revealed a big fat zero. None.

Not long afterward, hitting the phones again for a rug company, I somehow managed the exact same lack of success: no sale.

Since only a tiny slice of my life has involved buying or selling anything, I don't have a lot of examples to back my reliance on this reverse dictum of paying a high price and then selling cheap. Automobiles are among the few commodities that I've ever bought or sold. Used cars, to be precise. For the most part, *much*-used wrecks. A string of cheap, junk cars: tired old things that barely ran. At least, that's the condition they were in when I was ready to dispose of them.

Considering that I was almost invariably the final owner of the decrepit automobiles in question, they're not exactly a suitable example of business methodology, either.

As an antique auto enthusiast in the 1960s and 1970s, I possessed a couple of collectible, special-interest cars. Studebakers, mainly. Even though I've owned only a few automobiles of note, they do serve as examples of the incompetent trader's lack of art.

One of them, a 1963 Studebaker GT Hawk, deteriorated so much during my period of ownership that an acquaintance worried that if I stepped too hard on the gas, the body might fly right off the frame. Another Studebaker GT Hawk was in better shape when I finally sold it, for not too much less than I'd paid, having made only half-hearted attempts to repair some of its rust (which was not nearly as severe as the first one). Actually, I sold the two together, knowing that otherwise, no one would ever take the rusted-out hulk.

When I bought my 1936 Studebaker Dictator, I paid a price that would have been acceptable had the car been in good condition. The claims made by its owner for the car's mechanical integrity turned out to be false. Shortly after getting it home, I discovered that it was in desperate need of a complete brake overhaul, and had a lot of other smaller things wrong. (Incidentally, after 1937, the Studebaker company dropped the Dictator nameplate, in view of the fascist buildup toward war that was taking place in Europe.)

Selling the Dictator later, for close to what I'd originally paid (but not nearly what I had in it in terms of repairs), I wound up with two bidders. After a complicated three-way exchange, of the sort where everybody loses, the bidder who lost out was most displeased with me. So naturally, I ended the transaction feeling that I'd somehow cheated the person who didn't get it. Or maybe, both of them.

Around the same time, having never owned a convertible, I bought a 1967 Buick Skylark soft-top. How someone who supposedly knew something about cars could have purchased a vehicle as severely rusted-out as this one is a mystery. Having the gas tank almost fall off on a dusty rural road, due to drastic corrosion of its mounting straps, wasn't my finest hour of car ownership. I felt lucky to get anything at all for it when I sold it. In my defense, all I can say is that I was so taken with the notion of finally having a convertible, after craving one all my life, that I conveniently overlooked its numerous flaws.

In 1964, my mother inherited a pristine 1960 Studebaker Lark sedan, with only 4,000 miles on its odometer, from an elderly relative. Because Studebaker was about to go out of business, thus becoming more collectible, that car served as my gateway to auto writing. Except for the typical tendency of Studebaker bodies to rust, resulting in a need to replace the front fenders, it was in fine shape when sold in the 1970s, with low mileage. Nevertheless, I had a tough time getting a mere $600 for it.

My own next collectible looked a lot better than the two Studebaker Hawks, but also had a lot of Midwestern rust under the surface. This was a 1983 Chrysler LeBaron Mark Cross convertible: a lovely little machine with white paint, neat striping, and a rich leather interior. A nice-running engine, too. But a lot of rust underneath, thus not worth nearly as much as I'd paid.

Specifically, I'd bought it for $3,000; then, a few years later, sold it for $100, after a vandal broke the steering column and other parts while trying to steal it. This was among the first convertibles to reach the market after American automakers abandoned that body style in the mid-1970s.

For nearly all my other semi-collectible cars – which were just *old* cars when I had them – I was indeed the final owner, consigning them (sadly) to the crusher. On that forlorn list: a two-tone 1951 Pontiac hardtop; yellow/black 1950 Oldsmobile 88 hardtop; three step-down Hudsons; a pink/white Nash Ambassador with seats that folded into a bed (as well as back-fender rust that had been "repaired" using wood); a 1951 Buick Special.

My very first car, a 1948 Chevrolet coupe, was rusty with faded paint but ran well enough when purchased in the mid-1950s, soon after my 16th birthday. A few months later, I stupidly painted it in gray primer (with a brush), so it looked hideous. Coincidentally, for undiscovered reasons, its running condition got worse and worse, until the derelict little coupe died one night on a lonely highway.

Next came a dreary 1950 Chevrolet 150 two-door (the cheapest Chevrolet model of its time, when new), which looked and ran fine when I bought it. Until I painted it with grey primer, that is, using a vacuum cleaner this time, until it became worthless. Once again, to the crusher.

We've already heard about some of my most absurd car purchases, such as a Renault Dauphine that was missing a gear in its transmission and whose engine ran exactly two times before I got rid of it. Or, the Volvo PV544 with an engine that shook violently, due to a burned-out piston.

In stark contrast, friends and acquaintances who owned one collector car after another made money on nearly every one, typically having done little or nothing to them in terms of repair or restoration. They bought low and sold high; which, I do realize, is how it's supposed to work.

Ah yes, then there was the old house trailer, for which I paid $1,000. Had to chop down (okay, saw down) a small tree in order to move the trailer out of its original location. Because it had sat for many years, serving as a rest area for children attending a nursery school, I had no idea if the tires would hold up when attempting to move it to a campsite 200 miles away, in central Wisconsin.

Fortunately, a former girlfriend knew a fellow who specialized in hauling trailers. Amazingly, my quaint old relic of an early-day mobile home made the trip without a blowout or any other failure.

A couple of years later, I sold the trailer – ready for occupancy – to the campsite owner for $600. In addition to the original $1,000, I'd paid the cost of moving it and setting it up at the new location.

Regardless of the situation, I've felt guilty after every transaction, certain that I did something wrong to someone. Perhaps I wound up selling a car (or whatever else) to the least-deserving person, I didn't give the buyer sufficient information before the sale, and so on. Lots of reasons for guilt.

Regular business ventures turned out just as bad, though

missing the guilt element. When I established my own printed newsletter in 1993, promising helpful information to car-buyers, I had visions of making it a paying proposition. Never did I imagine what a futile effort that would become.

If only I could get a couple of hundred subscribers, I figured – perhaps even a thousand – I could get by without having to continue taking outside writing assignments. Well, I got subscribers all right, but they were barely measured in the dozens, at the publication's peak. Their annual subscription fees didn't come anywhere close to paying my printing and mailing costs. When I finally gave up the printed newsletter, I gave prorated refunds to all. And there weren't many.

I also had visions of selling what I wrote for the newsletter to other publications. Other journalists – professional and amateur alike – were doing this regularly. But despite all the promotional pieces I sent out, all the contacts I tried to establish, month after month, year after year, exactly one publication elected to republish something of mine. And never paid for it.

In the meantime, for a while, my newsletter began to pay off in a different way, at least temporarily. What is now one of the foremost online automotive publications, but was in the mid-1990s in its beginning stages, responded to one of my queries by offering to establish a tie with my newsletter if I put a version of it on the worldwide web, which was still in its formative stage. For each review or article that they linked to, I would get a modest – but much appreciated – payment.

That pleasant situation went on for three years. By then, that other publication had grown dramatically and was becoming a powerhouse in the field. So, the new editors decided my contributions were no longer needed, as they now had several staff members who could provide all the editorial matter that was required.

As a result, I was left with an online newsletter that had virtually no readers, producing no revenue whatsoever. Without a substantial readership, attracting advertisers was out of the question. But that was a blessing in disguise. During the late 1960s and 1970s, I'd worked in the lower echelons of the advertising business as a copywriter. At this point in my life, I wanted nothing to do with advertising.

So, I decided to abandon all thought of making my newsletter pay. As long as I was able to get enough outside work to provide a modest personal income, I'd keep producing the newsletter without any concern for financial remuneration. That's been its status since 1998. Shunning the advertising end was the best decision I could have made.

Though my career as an independent writer had its ups and downs, including some seriously lean years, I had a backup. From 1985 to 2012, I wrote the lion's share of the used car buying guide issued by a major publisher. No, it wasn't the most stimulating work imaginable, but it paid well enough, and probably served as my most useful contribution to consumer information. Used-car buyers needed plenty of help, and I welcomed the opportunity to help provide some guidance.

For five years (2001-05), I also wrote the entire vehicle buying guide for one of the fastest-growing automotive information sites. Not only was I paid for each group of reviews or articles that I wrote, but I received – for the first time in my life – a monthly retainer. Financially, this was the most stable and secure time of my entire life.

Then, late in 2005, the bottom dropped out. I was called into a meeting with the publisher, who'd brought in a cost-cutting expert. For more than an hour, I was pilloried by the two of them, questioned and accused as if I were in a police interrogation room. Only the bright light shining down in my face was absent. Why, they demanded, was I being paid both a retainer and separate fees for all my work? Because that's what was offered, I replied, over and over. I'd never asked for anything, never requested an increase; all I did was accept what had been freely proffered by the editors in charge at the time.

That was the end of my connection with them, but not the last time I had a regular monthly income – a wildly unbelievable bonus for any independent, freelance worker. Not long after the humiliating interrogation and loss of that five-year connection, I was hired by J.D. Power & Associates as one of the contributors to a new online buying guide. An annual fee was offered, to be paid in monthly installments. I couldn't have been more pleased, until they decided – at the end of the year – to drop the whole project, sending the whole group of us to the dustbin of unemployment.

Unfortunately, as the automobile business began to falter in 2008, writing assignments started to dwindle. Finally, late in 2012, I had to separate myself from my last client, because they'd announced an intention to change course drastically, with practices that I could not accept.

Unlike some independent colleagues, at least, I seldom had trouble being paid, though my initial experiences in the Sixties suggested caution. After stating my intention to leave my job as an industrial electronics copywriter, in order to attend the University of Illinois, that publisher offered to keep me on as a freelancer. That connection continued after graduation, until a few years later when checks stopped arriving. This time, the publisher wanted me to keep taking assignments, vowing to pay me eventually for everything. Unusually for me, as a generally meek person, I stood my ground and insisted on payment right then. And got it.

Meanwhile, my very first outside freelance writing assignment, way back in 1965, netted me nothing. This was a new little start-up company, and I was to get a whopping $20 for writing some ad copy. I stayed up all night to finish the project, then dashed downtown to drop it off early the next morning. Did I ever get my *twenty bucks*? I did not. Months later, I ran into a woman I knew who'd done considerably more work for this fellow. Evidently, he just gave up and disappeared.

For the next forty-plus years, on the other hand, I was incredibly lucky in terms of non-payment. Not until I decided a few years back that I needed some new clients did I get into trouble. I managed to attract three, and did some work for each (including six vehicle reviews for a new online magazine). All three companies promptly disappeared, paying nothing, and were never heard from again. So much for attracting new business.

Throughout my career, though, I've always managed to stay afloat, despite erratic income. That's mostly because I have a wife who is an expert at dealing with bills, matching them to income, no matter how uncertain the latter might be. I do my own taxes, too, and always have. Can't even imagine turning them over to someone else, who might be accustomed to a less-honest and precise approach to taxes, perhaps trying to stretch the rules in ways that I deplore as a citizen who believes in paying my fair share and nothing less.

Where my business-related incompetence lies is mainly my inability to promote myself, and to deal most effectively with clients that I happen to get. I detest negotiating and bargaining, always preferring that someone simply make me an offer, which I can either accept or refuse.

Things haven't gone any better when I've simply tried selling personal possessions. Back in 1980, when my wife and I decided to dispose of everything we had and move to Mexico for a time, we started taking all our stuff to flea markets and swap meets – especially those that dealt with automotive items. Eventually, we managed to get rid of everything, and it was sometimes even fun to function as a vendor, arriving at an event before dawn and setting up our selling tables.

At least, it's fun if you manage to sell a few things. What's really painful is to have a day of meager sales, then have to load up all that merchandise into the car for the trip back home.

One incident, though, demonstrates the incompetence that this book is all about. At a swap meet in Wisconsin, our car was parked along the edge of our selling space. That's how the area was laid out. After standing out there in the hot sun all day, we'd taken in something like $200. As we were packing up, getting ready to leave, I backed the car out of our space – and immediately ran over a stack of chrome trim strips that were lying on the ground at the next vendor's space, protruding right up to the edge of ours. As a result, I wound up paying him every cent we'd taken in that day, to compensate for the damage done to his chrome pieces. Net earnings for a day's work: zero.

Some years later, I went with a friend to sell at a popular swap meet in northern Illinois. We set no records for sales, but took in enough to make the day worthwhile. A year later, we went to the same event. Things had changed. Buyers were absent, and we were almost alone in this huge enclosure, which held only about half a dozen vendors in all. After standing at our sales table all day, we didn't even take in enough to pay for the rental of the space.

My most recent foray into the business world shows every evidence of being the same sort of fiasco. Because my office was packed full of old automotive printed materials, I decided to try and get rid of many or most them, by becoming an eBay seller. I took a class in eBay operations, and joined a Meetup group of Chicagoland sellers. At the monthly meetings, members told of their phenomenal successes, buying merchandise cheaply – often in quantity – and reselling each item on eBay for substantially higher figures.

My own efforts were far less fruitful. After a couple of years of trying, I'd managed to sell barely two dozen items, after listing hundreds for sale. Most of the sales, too, brought in sums far below what I'd anticipated. I still have hopes of a turnaround, and of turning eBay into a source of retirement income. But when you have a history of nearly unbroken failure in every business venture attempted, the prospects don't seem particularly bright.

Can I interest you in a radio-controlled Mercedes-Benz model car? Maybe a set of Corvette photographs?

28

Money

"I have no job, no money, no prospects," wrote Henry Miller in his autobiographical novel, *Tropic of Cancer*. "I am the happiest man in the world."

Of course, the world was a bit different when those words were committed to paper. Henry Miller led a lusty expatriate life in Paris, in the 1920s and '30s. His days (and nights) were spent in colorful cafes, raucous bistros and racy brothels, not wandering the streets searching for a job or a handout. Honing his literary skills, Miller enjoyed the company of other rising stars in the arts who'd taken up residence in France.

Whether it's making money or handling it, I qualify as a full-fledged incompetent. Unlike Mr. Miller, I can hardly call myself "happy." But like him, I'm not terribly distressed about this particular form of incompetence, either. All told, I'm quite content with my financial life. My dissatisfactions with life rarely stem from economic woes of any sort.

On the other hand, for a person who's never cared much about money, at least not in recent decades, I've sure spent a lot of time and energy *worrying* about it, lamenting its absence, fretting about where my next dollar was coming from. That's an inevitable drawback to the freelance life, where a steady income is something that *other* people get.

Freelancers can do well one year, fall apart financially the next, and revive again in the next season. Or, those dismal years of few and unrewarding assignments can linger on and on, depending on what's happening out in the business world. And on pure chance.

Though worrying about money puts me in league with most

Americans, I differ from the majority in one crucial way: Unlike practically everyone in the universe, it seems, there's nothing I want. Nothing that can be bought with money, at any rate. In that respect, at least, I'm vastly more content than 99 percent of Americans, who seem to be constantly searching for ways to bring in more bucks. Not to mention the wealthy 1-percent, most of whom never seem satisfied with the largesse they already possess.

Evidently, money worries have never been an uncommon phenomenon. Even the prolific ancestor of communism, Karl Marx, spent much of his lifetime fretting about money and debt.

Actually, anyone who's been an independent worker, regardless of his or her political preferences, cannot help but worry about money. When there's never a steady flow of income, and you don't know where your next assignment is coming from – or if there will ever be one again – how can you help being anxious, at least a little, about your near-future?

All the more so for some, such as myself, who don't have the option of choosing to return to a regular job. After being without a "real" job since 1967, and now well into senior-citizenhood, the prospect of being hired for anything at all, even as an unpaid volunteer, falls far short of slim.

Especially in later life, though, I'm *far* more satisfied than most people with what I have. How many of us can make that claim, much less believe it?

One expatriate friend, despite earning a good income compared to the average in his region, worries and complains regularly about lack of money – past and present. Why? Most likely, because he knows that back in America, with degrees from prestigious universities, he'd be making considerably more in his chosen profession. Of course, he'd also be without the many advantages that he enjoys, living in a foreign country.

One highly successful author, who's penned and published hundreds of books for children and been paid well for them, nevertheless complains steadily that the publishing world has changed, and he's no longer earning anything. Or if an assignment comes along, the publisher offers only a modest, one-time fee for the work rather than the sizable royalties he'd long been accustomed to receiving. The fact that he lives most comfortably, and wants for nothing, is somehow readily ignored.

Once, after being pickpocketed in Barcelona, losing about $300 in cash along with a walletful of important cards that had to be replaced, I told a colleague what had happened. He was horrified. Not by the act itself, or the loss of credit cards and such, but by the theft of cold, hard cash. To him, the prospect of having $300 in cash snatched away was an unfathomable disaster. The fact that I basically shrugged it off simply added fuel to his fire of distress.

This same fellow has long been an avid Lotto player, spending countless dollars for the minuscule chance of getting rich. He's had a few sizable wins, too – once or twice, in the tens of thousands. But if you could add up how much he's played over the years, he's clearly well behind. That was certainly the case with my own father, a lifelong gambler who passed away at age 52 leaving nothing but gambling debts.

I, on the other hand, stopped buying lottery tickets years ago. Not so much because of the astronomical odds against each player, but because I don't wish to be rich. There, I said it. I don't want to be wealthy. What could be a more un-American statement than that?

When I was 13 or 14, my father gave me an envelope containing several hundred dollars – an awful lot of money in those days. I was told to take it to the Post Office and get a money order for that amount, so he could mail it to the company for which he worked as a part-time bill collector. Well, shades of future disasters in my life – and utterly unexpected escapes. Somewhere along the way, I dropped the envelope. Running home in a frenzy, I was prepared for the worst of punishments, and knew I deserved them.

Instead, some kind soul had found the envelope and brought it over to our apartment. I was saved. As I would be many, many times in my life – almost magically, by dumb luck – from a long string of mishaps. It's happened so many times that I can't believe it's all a coincidence. Somewhere out there, I must have some sort of guardian angel. A seriously patient angel, who never gives up on me, even after all these decades of stupid behavior.

    Unlike a lot of Americans, too, I have little admiration for the rich and absolutely no animosity toward the poor. I'd never dream of advising an unemployed person to "pull himself up by his bootstraps." I know better, partly from having worked as a public aid caseworker among the impoverished long ago, but also because I hold progressive political views that include a concern for the less-fortunate among us.

    Mainly, though, my empathy with the economically deprived stems from having had so much trouble myself finding jobs in my youth. If I had to deal with the kind of adversities most impoverished and disadvantaged people face in the hiring world, I'd never have gotten a job at all, and I know it. What I feel most about the poor is deep sadness, knowing that they are, of necessity, so totally focused on money because they have no choice.

    Compared to most, despite the overwhelming incompetence outlined in these pages, I've been blessed with good fortune. Despite a low and shaky income for most of my life, I've traveled extensively in Europe and Mexico, and even once to Japan. My work as an automotive journalist has taken me to events in places throughout North America that I'd never have imagined seeing on my own. I've laid my head on fluffy pillows in more luxury hotel rooms and suites than I could begin to count, nearly all of them paid for by one of the auto companies, when attending media programs to test-drive the new models.

    In addition, I've resided for several extended periods in foreign lands – mainly, in Mexico. And along the way, neither my wife nor I has ever missed a meal or had to sleep on a park bench. We've come close to destitution once or twice, but each time found a way out. Millions of others have not been so fortunate.

    What more could a person ask? Incompetent with money? Sure thing, my friend – and glad of it, too.

29

Public Speaking

Peering over the crowd in a banquet room at Chicago's sprawling McCormick Place, I could see dozens of familiar colleagues: journalists, PR people, auto-company executives. Also in the audience that morning were TV cameramen and on-air personalities, standing ready to hear and record my words.

It was opening day for media attendees at the Chicago Auto Show. I stood at the podium, overseeing that audience of several hundred, knowing that thousands of viewers might be watching my performance later that day, on the local evening news. This was the keynote breakfast, sponsored by the Chicago Automobile Trade Association and the Midwest Automotive Media Association, affectionately known as MAMA.

On this particular occasion, I was president of MAMA. As such, my duties included presiding over that yearly auto-show breakfast meeting, welcoming the guests, and explaining the agenda for the occasion.

Oddly enough, I wasn't petrified. Nor frightened. I wasn't even all that tense.

Actually, I was amazed to discover that I could do it at all, much less without reading a script. All I had were brief notes. My worst fear – of becoming totally mute when the TV cameras and microphones were pointed in my direction – didn't happen. In fact, I rather enjoyed the occasion, which is most emphatically not how I'd dealt with public speaking earlier in my life. Afterward, two colleagues with histories as radio/TV personalities praised my laid-back performance. I couldn't have been more pleased.

By that time in my life, I'd already found my inner "ham," though I'd never imagined that a shy, painfully bashful person such as myself could have one. I found it by appearing a couple of times on radio shows as an expert on automotive matters. But more so, in the late 1990s, when I became a fairly frequent guest commentator on WGN-TV, a station that broadcast not only in Chicago but was seen all over the country – and beyond. Working with a delightfully spirited young woman, Robin Baumgarten, who normally did the morning traffic reports but periodically put together an automotive piece for the evening news show, I turned in some credible guest performances for the small screen. And I still have tapes of some of those episodes to prove it.

Years earlier, during an ill-fated semester spent in Law School, I had to participate in moot court: a simulated courtroom where students presented a case based upon real-world legal principles and precedents. We had about two months to prepare our case, working in teams of two. Then, each of us would appear before a judicial panel to argue its merits.

As was my shameful practice in those days, I wrote the legal brief during the night before it was due, actually *running* to the Law School building to drop it into the professor's mailbox before the 2:00 p.m. deadline.

A few weeks later, during the actual moot court session, I knew next to nothing about the case. Yet, I had to appear, and I did. To make things easier, I planned to outline the basic facts of the case, about which I had at least a cursory knowledge. My partner was far more serious a student, well prepared to delve into the meatier aspects of the case.

Unfortunately, the chief judge stopped me almost at the start, acknowledging that the panel already knew the facts and starting to pelt me with questions. How I responded, I don't know. Whether any of my answers made sense, or had anything to do with the case at hand, I couldn't say. We weren't graded on the court presentation (only on the written paper accompanying it), so I can't say for sure if I failed as miserably as I assumed I did. The only reaction I ever received was from one of the judges, who declared that I'd been "poised under pressure." Well, I don't know about the poised part, but I certainly felt the pressure that day.

During that court session, I reacted as I always do under tense situations: as if someone else were doing the actual speaking, and I was standing a bit to the rear, just watching leisurely. That's how I've always coped with such difficult tasks.

Upon receiving my B.A. from the University of Illinois, after starting and stopping my college career three times, I'd hoped to go to graduate school. My goal: to get a Master's in Labor and Industrial Relations. But I had no funds, and the small grant that had helped me get through undergraduate years ended with the one degree.

Just as well, though, because I'd have been sitting there petrified all through graduate school. Why? Because of the need to orally "defend" your thesis or dissertation. No matter how carefully I might have prepared such a document (and I was most definitely not known for intense studying while in college), I'd have been so petrified by the thought of facing an academic committee that I'd probably have run out of the room and headed for the nearest bar. The one that serves drinks, not the one that lawyers belong to. At least, that would have been my fear.

Now and then, I've somehow managed to do better than I'd thought. Employment interviews were always horror stories, partly because I'd become tongue-tied and incommunicative. (In recent times, I'm more inclined to blabber on – but again, as if another person is doing the actual talking.)

After moving to southern California in the mid-1960s, following a 14-month stint as a public aid caseworker in Chicago, I applied for several social work jobs. Orange County had me come in for an oral interview. I was in a state of panic. Not only was I fearful of speaking, as usual, but I'd had a passel of personal problems when I'd left Chicago, and they weren't getting any better out in the west.

Following that interview, conducted by a group, I was absolutely convinced that it was a disaster. Surely, I'd been the worst, least capable candidate they'd ever encountered. When I heard nothing further from them, and eventually gave up on

California and headed back to the midwest, that impression was affirmed.

Then, weeks after my return to Chicago, I got a letter asking me to show up at work in Orange County on a particular date. I couldn't believe it. Surely this had to be an error. Going back to California wasn't an option at that time, but I was flabbergasted that anyone on that interview panel could have given me a passing mark as a possible candidate for the job. To this day, that letter ranks as one of the biggest – and most satisfying – surprises of my life, even though I never followed up on the offer.

At my mother's funeral in 2005, I gave a short eulogy. I was in my 60s at the time. Good thing, too, because just a few years earlier, I wouldn't have been able to stand up there and speak, even to this tiny funeral-home audience.

So, why was I so incompetent at public speaking for most of my life? In addition to basic shyness, it was an utter lack of self-confidence. Yet, as that moot court judge pointed out, I could somehow exhibit poise when under fire, in the midst of frantic inner tensions.

The fact that I've always spoken softly, and often cannot be heard, hasn't helped, either. On the other hand, when living in a hotel years ago, I was told by the telephone operator that I had an appealing phone voice. She was obviously in a position to know; and she wasn't the only person who'd said such a thing. Regardless, my perception of inability to speak acceptably well could not be extinguished.

Even today, though, I'm petrified by the thought of encountering TSA officers at the airport, or immigration/customs officials when entering a foreign country. I'm always afraid I'll become mute, and certain that I look guilty of something. That's how I invariably appear in my own mind, if not necessarily to everyone I meet out in the real world.

30

Learning and Teaching

"If you can't do, teach." That little saying has been around for a long time, despite its being a gross oversimplification. Teaching is a marvelous occupation, which should be held in the highest regard. What could possibly be more important, more inwardly rewarding, than imparting morsels of knowledge, confidence – perhaps even an occasional bit of wisdom – to young people?

Unless you're as inadequate at teaching as you are at doing, that is. What if you're incompetent at both?

In this instance, I never even *attempted* to teach, because my potential incompetence was so obvious. After all, in addition to an ability to convey information orally, don't you need to *know* something in order to teach it? Since I perceive myself as knowing nothing, I wouldn't dream of inflicting my lack of knowledge upon students of any age, at any learning level. They deserve far better.

All my life, the very idea of teaching, of standing in front of a class, has been a major fear, whether that means talking to kids, teens, adults, or old folks. To be blunt, I'd be terrified of my students, regardless of their age or academic level.

What could I possibly say to a group of students of any sort, I would invariably ask myself. Even for a subject with which I was familiar, whatever little I might know just cannot be transmitted orally. Not from my lips. Which, of course, is precisely why I became a writer. At least, I possess *some* degree of competence with the printed word.

I'm invariably reminded of the movie *Starting Over*, with Burt Reynolds as a grizzled newsman who agrees to teach a journalism class. As he finishes his remarks at the end of the first class, he tells the students that they'll be continuing tomorrow. Then, he looks up at the wall clock. Five minutes have passed since he began speaking to the class, and he's run out of material. I've empathized with that tortured look on his face many a time.

The prospect of teaching is one reason (though hardly the only one) why I never got more than a couple of credits in graduate school. In addition to facing the prospect of oral examinations along the way, attaining a graduate degree would have opened up the possibility of trying to teach, and that's an inconceivable occupation in my mind.

How *anyone* can stand in front of a classroom – whether it's kindergartners, postgrad students, kindly grandmothers, or any group in between – and talk for hours, or even for minutes, is an utter mystery. What can they possibly have to say, about anything? Why isn't their mind a complete blank?

Because of my own inability to convey knowledge by voice and actions, I am in awe of teachers. In my view, they deserve the highest possible salaries and recognition of their value to society. Not so much the professors in higher education, many of whom appear to lead a relatively cushy life that requires only a minimum of actual in-class educating. As anyone who's spent time in a university knows, too, not everyone with a professorial title is adept at effectively transmitting his or her knowledge to students.

No, my admiration focuses on the less-renowned, overworked and underpaid public-school teachers: the ones who, often against all odds, strive to turn our young people into knowledgeable, upstanding participants in the world around them. No one deserves recognition and rewards more than they. Yet, they've become the villains in an anti-labor drama perpetrated by politicians who castigate the public sector, and especially the unions that represent those workers.

(As an explanatory aside, impostors, who are unqualified to teach when measured by ordinary standards, typically do so by simply staying a chapter ahead in the textbook. They can do this because they're able to teach themselves by reading, then convey what was learned only minutes or hours before to others.)

Lack of teaching skills is only part of the problem. I was among the world's worst students, too. Few knew my secret, including elementary and high-school teachers, some of whom praised my work profusely.

Throughout my school days, I'm compelled to admit, I was a test-passer, not a student. I seldom took books home. I did as little homework as possible, and then only in study hall. At the most, I'd carry my current math textbook home, because I rather enjoyed those problems – especially in algebra.

Basically, in grade school and high school (though less so in college), I was nearly always able to discern just how little really needed to be studied in order to pass – and to get a relatively high grade at that.

Virtually all that I know, I learned on my own, by reading and observing. I cannot recall any teacher who was particularly inspiring, or who stimulated much in the way of love of learning. Not past Kindergarten, at any rate. In fact, I find it a bit odd when well-known authors and others look back upon their childhoods and youth, and nearly always can point to a specific teacher who helped them become what they are today.

My lack of devotion to learning was mainly a result of sheer laziness on my part, definitely; but probably also involved a touch of what would today be called Attention Deficit Disorder. Even when reading a newspaper today, I seldom go all the way to the end of a story, or anywhere near, unless it's written by a columnist I really like and enjoy. Otherwise, I get bored part way through, and feel I already have grasped the gist of the piece.

Psychologists and physicians would probably disagree, since I've never been tested for such maladies, but I also believe I've long had a touch of dyslexia, as well as autism (most likely, of the Asperger's Syndrome variety). All I can say is that I've experienced a lifetime of mild but observable symptoms that are consistent with each of those phenomena.

Regardless, looking back, I am mortified and ashamed for having wasted all those years in school, gleaning so little and expending so little effort.

Incompetent

Being essentially a writerly person, I work with words continuously – but only the printed version, not oral. I could write a fine lesson plan for teaching any subject I'm familiar with, and probably for some that I know little about. But ask me to stand in front of a class and talk about even the most elementary aspects, and you may as well be requesting me to wade across a swamp that's filled with hungry, teeth-baring alligators.

31

Telephones and Communication

In this age of constant, incessant phone communication – with seemingly everybody buried in a smart phone whenever they're awake – could there be someone who detests telephones? Who rarely uses them?

How about one who feels totally inept when it comes to telephonic communication – yet doesn't feel the least bit guilty or inadequate about that failing.

Yes, there could be such a person, and my hand is raised emphatically to claim that title. Not only do I disdain cell phones, I have little use for telephones of *any* kind, including the landline at home.

For most of my life, I've dreaded making calls. Even simple ones. For instance, changing a flight reservation. Or, ordering pizza delivery. And *receiving* calls – just hearing that phone ring – causes even greater distress. In my view, the answering machine was one of the greatest inventions ever, allowing persons such as myself to let most, if not all, calls be dealt with automatically.

For one thing, I've always worried that the other party would find fault with what I was asking, or with my response. Mainly, though, I simply have no interest in phoning, and certainly not in doing so via cell phone.

Talk to whom? Call whom? Practically nobody calls *me*, which is A-1 as far as I'm concerned. I call almost no one. That's also fine with me. With a few exceptions for one or two special people, only rarely is there even a hint of joy in phone conversations. For years, too, I've managed to "train" my clients and occupational contacts to communicate with me only by e-mail, not by telephone.

Incompetent

Working as a journalist, doing interviews is part of my job – but certainly not a favorite part. I don't conduct interviews nearly as often as most people in the media, but they have to be done at least occasionally. Colleagues sometimes proclaim how they're able to induce interviewees to reveal great secrets, which would otherwise go unsaid, because of the interviewer's talent for drawing out information from reluctant people. Because they're so skillful at interviewing techniques, the interviewee winds up saying more than intended.

I, on the other hand, have a tough enough time getting interviewees to tell me what they *want* to make public.

Doing phone interviews as a journalist also is difficult for two tangible reasons. First, it's hard to take notes when people talk so fast on the phone, which impairs my ability to keep up. Secondly, and more important, is the inability to see reactions in the person, which can be more revealing than what's actually being said. There's also the constant worry that I'll lose my place and get hopelessly lost, leading to awkward pauses and probably to sheer embarrassment. A moment's hesitation and my mind is likely to go blank, with no idea what's been said, or what to ask next.

Mainly, though, I'm just plain uneasy and nervous on the phone. Also, I dislike my phone voice, and I tend to run out of breath due to tension. Yet, that telephone operator at Chicago's old Hotel Lincoln, where I lived for two years many years ago, praised my voice and found it appealing. Others have said so, too.

Only occasionally have I encountered people whose distaste for phone work matched or approached mine. One was a young woman who worked next to me at a printing company, back in the Sixties. Periodically, she'd ask me to make calls that she'd been requested to do. Perhaps it was because she spoke with a light foreign accent, but she obviously felt even more uncomfortable with a mouthpiece in front of her than I did.

Long before "smart" phones, too, telephones were at least simple to operate. Whether operated by rotary dial or, later, a set of 12 large pushbuttons, the procedure wasn't nearly as intimidating as it is today – at least for the phonophobic among us. Now, phones are obligated to use tiny touch screens that only a techie should be able to manipulate. Yet, these oppressive little devices are in the hands of countless folks who have no idea how the cell-phone system works. Nor do they care, as long as it lets them chatter constantly to their sea of friends, relatives, cohorts, lovers, and whoever else occupies a part of their lives.

A dreadful admission is necessary here. At one time, not so long ago, I did possess a cell phone. I was living in France for nearly two months, and my hostess insisted that a cell phone would be virtually essential. So, I agreed to obtain one, with her help. If memory serves, I used it twice during that time span. Worse yet, only with considerable difficulty was I able to figure out how to use it – and that was only partially due to the instructions being printed in French.

Adding insult to injury, the cell-phone provider somehow assumed that I was eager to get up-to-the-minute results of the rugby matches taking place at that time. Several times a day, as late as 11 p.m., the phone would ring and a text message with the latest scores appeared on the screen. If I had any love for cell phones, it would have evaporated every time I heard that late-night ring, announcing information that did not interest me in the least.

If you're an avid cell-phone user (and who isn't these days, except for a few diehards like myself), watch out. If I were to come into power, one of my first actions would be to eradicate all phones from the known universe. So, better hang onto your smart phone if you hear that I'm running for office, before I come and snatch it away.

32

Driving

Wait a minute. What's *this* one doing here? How can driving be an example of incompetence, when I've spent the major share of my career as a writer and journalist covering the automobile business. Cars and driving go together, don't they?

For most auto writers, yes, they do. But not for all. And definitely not for me, despite almost three decades as a professional journalist, evaluating the road behavior of cars of every sort.

Unlike nearly every auto journalist I've encountered, I make no claim whatsoever to be more than an average driver. Perhaps not even that capable, now that I'm into senior-citizenhood and the marginal skills I've employed all these years aren't working quite as well anymore.

It wasn't always so. As a teenager, I did exhibit a certain level of skill. At least, I thought I did. Looking back, a lot of that evidence of capability, displayed by foolishly stupid, high-risk driving sessions, was illusory. Not to mention dangerous.

Most teenagers in the 1950s could hardly wait to get their driver's licenses, and I was no exception. The day I turned 16, I was at the Illinois department of motor vehicles, taking the test.

Since I'd never had an instruction permit, how could I pass a driving test? (Sensitive readers, who insist on total compliance with the law, are advised to skip the next couple of paragraphs.) I'd actually been driving regularly for the previous two years, without benefit of a license. My father didn't like to drive, but needed to get around Chicago and suburbs for his part-time job as a bill collector for a magazine subscription company. Therefore, starting at age 14, he agreed to let me drive him around his route.

Once I turned 15, he tried to get me a license under the

Driving

"hardship" provision that permitted an exception to the usual minimum age. The state of Illinois did not accept his request, but I kept driving regardless. Actually, just before I'd become 15, Illinois changed its minimum age for licensing from 15 to 16; so, I almost felt I was *entitled* to drive despite the current regulation.

Fortunately, I was never stopped by a police officer who might disagree with that rationalization. I managed to evade the law even when I snuck the car keys out of my father's pocket, while he was asleep in the early morning, so I could drive his car around the neighborhood. One time, I thought I was in for trouble when the car stalled as I drove up a slight incline; but I managed to get it started again and leave that scene.

Good fortune also prevailed during an outing with a more serious outcome. One evening when I was 15, after persistent nagging on my part, my father agreed to let me take his car to my friend's house, even though it was only a block away. Little did he know that I planned to take a group of friends out driving. Nor did he (or I) realize that an ice storm was starting, which would soon turn into one of the worst in Chicago's history. After going a few miles with my group of teenage boys, the ice turned treacherous. Even though I'd done considerable driving by that time, I lacked the experience to deal with the prospect of skidding. Sure enough, when trying to apply the brakes at an underpass, I slid right into the back end of another car.

This was not a proud moment in my teenage life, but it was certainly a frightening one. No one was hurt at all, but both cars were damaged – my father's, worst of all. We all waited for the police to arrive on the scene of the accident. And waited, and waited. Meanwhile, I'd found a public phone nearby and called my father, to explain what had happened. He and I had our differences in those days, to say the least. But I am amazed to this day by his actions on that icy night. Instead of berating me over the phone, and later at home, he got dressed and walked a block to get on a city bus, heading for the accident scene.

When he got there, instead of starting to scream at me, as

expected, he quietly said to me, simply, "Fade." In Chicago parlance, that meant get out of here, right now. Which I did. Because of the severe ice on the streets, accidents had taken place all over the city that night, and the police were grossly behind in their attempts to get to each one.

While I made my way out of the scene, he got behind the wheel of his injured 1948 Dodge, started the engine, and backed away from the car with which he'd collided. Yes, he left the scene of an accident. But if I was breaking the law by driving without a license, he was doing likewise by virtue of driving while intoxicated.

Without question, both of our actions were shameful: mine and his. But if nothing else, that incident instilled within me a deep respect for the dangers of icy pavement, which I carry with me to this day. It also helped stimulate an aversion to breaking the law, marred only by a few years of driving at excessive speeds in my late teens and 20s.

During those adolescent and early-adult years, on the other hand, I was admittedly a menace on Chicago streets. So were a lot of other male drivers of my age; but that's hardly an excuse for all the bad motoring behavior I exhibited, nearly every time I got behind the wheel.

Once licensed, and especially after buying the first of my long string of jalopies and clunkers, I began driving not only faster than prudence should have dictated, but way more recklessly. I drove my old wrecks as if they were high-performance muscle machines or sports cars. They weren't. To this day, I cannot believe I survived those risky high-speed runs on bald tires, in cars with shaky steering or tremulous suspensions.

A typical outing involved taking precarious chances, clearly exceeding my limitations. Friends began to refer to me as "swift-shift," pointing to my prowess at manipulating the column-mounted gearshifts used on cars of the 1950s. Little did they know that gear-shifting was practically my only true skill on the road.

Drunken driving also came to the forefront, I'm ashamed to admit, soon after tasting alcohol for the first time. I was a few weeks short of my 17th birthday, and that first drink led to many, many more over the next 15 years.

Thank heavens, I managed to avoid hurting anyone. But I did get myself in trouble, shortly after starting Law School. I quit after the first semester, mainly because I'd abruptly realized on the first day of class that the law was not for me, and I was in the wrong place. But that decision also was influenced by the debacle that I created by getting behind the wheel at the end of a drunken party. Again, no one was hurt, but partygoers who imprudently chose to accompany me in my 1954 Hudson did not finish the night in a joyful frame of mind.

No, I never got into real street racing, of the sort pictured in movies depicting the California car culture, from *Rebel Without a Cause* in the Fifties to the *Fast and Furious* series in more recent times. But I did drive aggressively and foolishly, either unaware of or in denial of my roadgoing limitations.

Thankfully, while still in my 20s, I realized how foolish it was. Though I'd occasionally step harder on the gas than I should have over the next few years, by my mid-30s, that part of my life was over.

Many years later, when driving a Mini Cooper with a fellow journalist at a West Coast media event, he mentioned that every time he got into a new car, he wanted to drive off as fast as possible. This was no kid, but a man of roughly my own age. "Oh, I got over that a long time ago," I informed him. He was amazed, his face displaying shocked disbelief.

More and more, when attending media drive programs, I got sick and tired of the dangerous driving I'd witness. When I first began as an auto journalist, I'd been warned to avoid certain driving partners who were well known for their notoriously high-risk habits. One local journalist told me about riding with a stranger in the Pacific Northwest, hurtling down narrow logging roads at 140 miles an hour. We all had our lists of drivers who might be fine companions at dinner, but were to be avoided at all costs when behind the wheel.

Most amazing, some of the idiots would actually boast about their latest speeding tickets: both the ones they'd talked their way out of (by lying), and those they'd received. At one dinner, a particularly offensive moron who'd participated in a coast-to-coast race bragged that he did the most jail time of any driver involved at that event. How some of these journalists, menaces to themselves and everyone around them, were able to maintain their licenses, and their lives, is still a mystery. At least, I was not one of them.

Meanwhile, I had realized that my level of driving competence was no better than average, and in many ways fell well below the norm – especially for anyone in the auto business. This became particularly evident when driving on race tracks, which was often a part of media programs to promote a new car model. In no time, I realized that my foot-to-the-floor driving as a youth had demonstrated little beyond stupidity. Though I had friends who were exceptionally adept behind the wheel, comfortable even in the most challenging conditions, I was not one of them.

Despite hitting grossly illegal speeds through Chicago streets and even along dark, narrow alleys, I knew nothing of the ways to maintain control and get the most out of a vehicle. No one I knew had ever raced cars, and though I envied the guys that could, they were in another world.

On those race tracks as journalists, we were often paired with an expert race driver, who sat ready to point out our errors and deficiencies along the course. I must have been a trial to those racers, some of whom were relatively famous. Not only did I demonstrate only marginal skill at maneuvering the car through the curves and straightaways, but I failed to learn. Next time I tried, my performance was no better, and likely worse.

A few elements of my lack of skill couldn't be helped, and might have been attributable to something like dyslexia. At some of those media programs, the organizers would set up a barrier with three openings, side by side. Each of us in turn would drive toward the barrier, reaching 40 miles an hour or so. As we came close, aiming toward the center opening, a green light would suddenly go on, at either the left or right side. The idea was to suddenly twist the steering wheel in that direction, sailing through the correct opening and presumably affirming the handling capabilities of that particular car model.

Well, every time I tried – every single time – I'd wind up breezing through the wrong opening: the one that had a *red* light illuminated overhead. Even if I'd been driving at *walking* speed, I think I would have gotten it wrong.

Autocross events were a problem, too. Emphasizing fast, tight turns, these courses were laid out with cones to indicate the direction to follow at each juncture. Surprisingly, I wasn't the slowest driver going through a typical autocross – provided that I didn't get lost along the way. Something in my brain just didn't grasp the layout of cones that had been set up, so I was never quite sure whether to go right or left at the next corner. Not exactly the way to achieve a high score. Making matters worse, most autocross events were timed, with results displayed on a screen and/or announced afterward, so everyone would know how well – or how poorly – you did. Hardly the most comfortable situation for a minimally-talented driver who lacked confidence even for events in which he had a modicum of skill.

Off-road driving didn't go much better, though I never felt especially incompetent out on those unpaved pathways through forests and up mountain grades. Why? Because I found the whole concept to be silly. In my view, somebody invented paved roads so we wouldn't have to endure driving through the wilderness to get from one place to another.

Automakers who produce sport-utility vehicles, on the other hand, love to demonstrate how tough and controllable their products are, and what better way to do so than to have journalists drive them through the harshest terrain. The fact that only a minuscule handful of people who purchase those vehicles will ever leave the pavement is lost on those who enjoy wending their way through the most forbidding territory, even risking their lives traveling along high mountain ledges that provide barely enough space for a vehicle to maneuver.

Unlike most car enthusiasts, too, I never cared for long highway trips. When I drove alone from Chicago to southern California in 1965, the trip took eight days. Yes, I stopped for a while at several places along the way; but still, all I could average was about 300 miles a day. That was typical for me, even when other folks boasted of putting on 600, even 800, miles a day when on vacation. Friends used to drive from Chicago to Mexico, nonstop, sleeping in the car while someone else drove. I never wished to be along on those trips. On that California trek, incidentally, my worn-out 1958 Plymouth Plaza consumed something like 15 quarts of oil.

I was never that fond of driving at night, either. As for mountains, I never saw one until I made that California trip. Much later, my fear of heights made many a media driving program a horrific ordeal, because organizers loved to plan routes through some frightful, narrow mountain roads, often with heart-halting dropoffs alongside, and bereft of guard rails. On more than one occasion, I practically begged my driving partner to take the wheel during the most frightful segments.

Stints as a mail-truck driver and, a bit later, a UPS truck driver, demonstrated my lack of skill in other ways. Oh, I could handle the trucks well enough moving forward, though I wasn't quite as confident about fitting through narrow spaces as my fellow drivers seemed to be. Gearshifting was a breeze, when I was assigned a truck with a manual gearbox – even an old one that had unsynchronized gears.

What overtaxed my questionable capabilities, though, was backing up a truck – even a small one. At one loading dock, a worker warned me that I'd almost hit the entry pillar as I backed my UPS truck into its space. Naturally, I was offended, to be called out like that. But he was right.

Years later, one of the monthly events held by the Midwest Automotive Media Association, when I was an officer of that group, took place at a truck-driving school. I'd never even attempted to drive a semi-trailer truck before. Even my well-founded skill at shifting gears failed me on that occasion. Worst of all, though, were my attempts to back up that beast into a simulated loading dock, using only the truck's outside mirrors. Good thing I wasn't out in the real world in the cab of a loaded semi, struggling to back it into a loading/unloading space. Traffic would have been tied up for miles, waiting in vain for me to get it right at long last.

Despite my distaste for driving, and especially for the growing lot of drivers misbehaving on today's roads, my love for classic and special-interest cars has not disappeared. It's just faded a bit into the background, at a time in history when far more important matters vie for attention.

So, yes, an occasional sighting of a 1935 Auburn Speedster, a 1937 Cord convertible, or a 1941 Lincoln Continental still gets my heart fluttering. So do Alfa Romeos, Fiat roadsters, Morris Minors, Jaguar XK-120s, early Mini Coopers, Citroen 2CVs, 1950s Studebaker coupes, and ever so many more examples from the past, ranging from the exotic and rare down to the simply unique and intriguing. Beautiful they all are, as mementos of the automotive arts; but my innate enthusiasm is emphatically tempered by a realization of the damage that the entire car culture has done to all of us.

My wife, incidentally, owned exactly one automobile during her youth, and it was among the most coveted models from the Fifties: a 1957 Bel Air convertible, in turquoise and white. She owned it in the Sixties, when special-interest cars had not yet become sought-after. At the time, it was just a nice old car, which she sold for a few hundred dollars – a reasonable figure for the period. No wonder the two of us seemed to have such a unique affinity when we met and got together, years after that Bel Air was sold.

33

Having Fun

"Are we having fun yet?" We've all heard that toss-off query from some sardonic or hypercritical soul, intended to dismiss and scoff at the pleasures of whatever is taking place at the moment.

For some of us, the question rarely warrants a "yes." Life simply isn't much fun. Mostly, no fun at all. In fact, for some of us, fun is a foreign concept; while for others, it's practically the purpose of life.

There's a psychiatric term for the inability to have fun: *anhedonia*. More specifically, it's defined as the inability to experience pleasure.

I definitely do not suffer from anhedonia. It's not that total. I've experienced fun. Pleasure, too. Even excitement, sensation, joy. Just not all that often, and seldom for long. And not for many years, now that I'm a senior citizen. Needless to say, I'm not one of those seniors depicted on some TV commercials, spending his days on joyful pursuits and smiling all the time.

More important, nearly every sensation of fun has been accompanied by so much worry, tension, and especially "what-ifs," that any basic pleasure gets lost in the morass. It's a bit like a young fellow going on a date, who is ordered to bring his nasty little brother along – an appendage guaranteed to impede any romantic progress.

Something like 99 percent of the time, every hint of pleasure and joy is marred by concern, care, and dread. Not much of a way to go through each day.

More annoying yet, it's difficult even to *fantasize* about fun, because dark clouds of worry and foreboding immediately creep into the picture, tainting whatever pleasures might be imagined.

During my early adulthood, a friend used to refer to "the happy people," making it clear that he (and presumably I) were not among them. Not everyone falls fully on one side or the other, but most of us do have a tendency to be either happy much of the time, or unhappy a lot of the time.

Sports and games aren't much fun when you know you're going to lose – and lose big. How could it be otherwise, when your entire previous life demonstrated a propensity to come in last, or close to it, at everything you attempted. Hobbies and crafts aren't fun either, when you "know" the result of your efforts will be mediocre at best, based upon past efforts, and quite possibly reach the level of embarrassment.

Conversations, of course, aren't fun if you're bashful, tongue-tied, and/or anxious. As for parties and gala events of any sort, way back in my drinking days, disastrous results were a likely outcome. Most likely, under the influence of considerable quantities of alcohol, I'd do something embarrassing, humiliating, or just plain stupid. Although I'd appear to be having fun, that sensation was obviously illusory, fueled solely by alcohol.

After becoming sober and remaining so, on the other hand, I attended few social gatherings except in the course of my work. And many of those weren't much fun. Watching others have what must have been fun became my role, though it didn't always look all that joyful.

Not everybody needs or wants a life based largely upon fun, upon pleasure. But we can all use at least a little bit of it. Without the prospect of occasional fun, what reason can there be to get up every morning?

During one episode of the old *Lou Grant* TV show, the fictional newspaper's managing editor refers to the problems faced by a new, young character seeking to become a reporter, who had obvious mental troubles. "There's no joy in his life," he explained to Ed Asner, who portrayed the title character. I've often wondered how many people in the viewing audience grasped the full significance of that statement.

Long ago, I spent a New Year's Eve driving aimlessly around the city with a friend of sorts. Both of us proclaimed that we'd never allow such a thing to happen again: we'd make sure to have someplace to go on such a celebratory occasion. I can't speak for his future partygoing activities; but for me, most holidays in the succeeding half-century were indeed spent alone. Or, on the rare occasion when I've been invited to an event, watching from the sidelines as the others enjoyed themselves. One big difference: I'm not nearly as bothered by that inability to participate as I used to be.

34

Writing

During half a century as a full-time professional writer, working independently, I've earned my entire living with words. Printed words at first, then words on a screen. Yet, silly as it sounds, I have to admit to a striking level of incompetence even in this area: even in what I do best.

Becoming an independent writer did provide one monumental benefit. It allowed me to find a way to earn a living without having to endure the stress and anxiety of going to a regular job each day. For a nervous, anxious person who's uncomfortable around people, having to spend entire days at a desk in some office, not to mention commuting each day, would have constituted perpetual mental torture. Normal people put up with it; excessively anxious people try and avoid that kind of regular life. In this respect, I have been incredibly lucky. Had I not discovered this occupational option, I cannot begin to imagine what the last half-century of my life would have been like.

As an independent worker for so long, I've definitely had my ups and downs. Reasonably good years and terrible ones. Even during the dry spells, with little (sometimes no) money coming in for long periods, my wife and I managed to stay afloat financially. We never missed a meal (in fact, a glance at our respective girths suggests that we might have benefitted from missing one now and then). We've lived simply, but comfortably enough. We never owned property of any kind, but that's been largely a personal choice. We have no assets other than our 5-year-old car, which was leased when new and subsequently purchased, but we don't feel deprived in the least. That was our first new car ever – and my first one that didn't qualify as decrepit.

On the plus side, we have no debts and always manage to pay our bills. We reside in a studio apartment (one L-shaped room plus a full, but small, kitchen and ample bathroom). For us, it's exactly the right size. Until going on Medicare a few years back, we were without health insurance for nearly two decades, due to pre-existing conditions. Yet, when my wife needed a hip replacement, and the cost had to be paid in cash, we found a way to comply.

In short, writing for a living has been good to me. Though I've never had the kind of earnings that big-time authors take in, or anything close, we've survived well; and I'm more than aware that being able to earn a passable living as a freelancer for close to fifty years is almost unheard-of. Most freelancers give it up long before approaching that sort of time frame.

And yet, I consider myself an abject failure as a writer. Yes, millions of my words have been published; but in my view, most of them were worthless words. Why? Because they were about automobiles, not issues of any importance to the world. Rather than looking back upon a successful and worthwhile life, I see mine as dominated by rejection, poor choices, and ultimate failure.

In fact, I once considered submitting my record of rejections to the Guinness Book of World Records. But it turned out that there were plenty of contenders for any list of regularly-rejected authors. It's a safe bet, though, that few others – if any – have actually earned their livings for most of a lifetime by turning out words.

I began submitting manuscripts and proposals to magazine publishers in 1961, while I was a voluntary resident of a mental hospital in Chicago. I'd signed myself in at age 22, diagnosed as suffering from "anxiety and panic reaction," no longer able to cope with the everyday world. Especially the workaday world. During my 3½-month stay at the hospital, writing occupied a substantial amount of my time.

At first, I submitted short stories. Later, non-fiction articles. Over the next 50 years, I can't begin to estimate how many submissions I made, of full manuscripts and modest proposals. Not a single one was ever bought and published. None. Zero.

Yet, throughout that entire half-century, I've earned my living

Writing

almost totally as an independent writer. Haven't had a "real" job since 1967. Even though nobody ever wanted my words of fiction or what I considered serious non-fiction, a long string of publishers happily paid me for my efforts when writing about electronic equipment, turning out catalog and mail-order advertising copy; and then, starting in 1975, writing about automobiles.

I got into that latter field by writing articles about antique and classic cars (a personal interest since childhood), along with how-to pieces related to auto repair and maintenance. Then, after a few years, I evolved into covering new and used cars, and the auto business, as a full-fledged and at least moderately recognized journalist. Along the way, I had more than two dozen books published – mostly about collectible cars and automotive history, but also including six books for children.

So, even though I've been a reasonably successful writer in a niche market, earning a respectable and adequate income most of the time (with some seriously lean years along the way), do I consider myself the least bit successful?

Absolutely not. Nowhere near. I see myself as a dismal failure, unable to get a single work of any consequence into print.

That's why I started my own website in 1995: so there would always be a place for what I write. But since it's never had more than a tiny trickle of readership, and I've confined it largely to automobiles (until recently), it's never been much of a step ahead of not being published at all.

Nowadays, of course, a 10-year-old kid can put a video on YouTube or some newer equivalent and have thousands, even millions, of viewers in a matter of hours (if not minutes). In a single day, a kid like that gets more viewers/readers than I've attracted in an entire lifetime of writing and publishing.

For many of my journalist colleagues, auto writing has been a monumentally satisfying occupation. At one time, it was for me as well. In addition to having our words published and relied upon by car-shoppers and owners, and being paid at least passably well in the process, we've gotten to drive the latest models well before they go on sale. Many of us have been on the invitation lists of most auto manufacturers, urged to attend preview drive events all over the country. And for some, all over the world. Though I've only rarely been asked to attend international events, I've driven a Jaguar in France, a Lexus in Austria, and GM SUVs in Mexico, as well as countless cars in Canada.

My colleagues and I also have stayed in more four- and five-star hotels than we could count, nearly always courtesy of one auto company or another. Journalists employed by major newspapers and some other organizations are not permitted to accept paid-for business trips, but those of us who are independent or work for secondary publications have no such prohibition. In so doing, I've accumulated more than a million frequent-flyer miles on a single airline, personally enjoying the benefits that accrue from achieving elite status.

So, what could I possibly be complaining about? That's easy. In my opinion, writing about cars is trivial, meaningless, and unsatisfying. Not to mention the fact that it's contributing, by encouraging automobile use, to environmental pollution and waste of precious fossil fuels.

Even more important, I consider the automobile to be a major contributor to the decline in civility and courtesy in modern society. It's also a worrisome example of elements of conspicuous consumption, and the foremost reason for excessive suburban development and overcrowding, as well as the need for lengthy commutes. In short, I don't like cars nearly as much as I used to.

At first, auto-writing was compelling, and tempting. But the glow began to wear off after a few years. In those early days, a byline was always welcome, no matter what kind of publication offered it, and for what topic it was granted. Later, I came to realize how inconsequential the auto business was, and how the car culture was making our world worse instead of better in a troubling number of ways. Whatever pleasure I used to derive from turning in my work was rapidly fading away.

At that point, the writing assignments began to sink into uninterrupted drudgery – the kind that, truth be told, most workers experience for part, if not all, of their working lives. Little sense of accomplishment, no feeling of purpose. Apart from the tiny twinges of delight that come when you create a particularly well-turned phrase, or the equivalent in any other occupational endeavor, it's nothing at all.

So, why were all my "important" pieces and proposals rejected or ignored, by hundreds of editors at publications of all sorts? Obviously, I'll never know. Something about my choice of subject matter, or my way of treating each subject, just never caught the eye and imagination of editors who make those decisions. As a result, what I'd once hoped would be a satisfying worklife turned into a lifetime of rejection and disappointment, eased moderately by the meager "success" of lingering for so many years as an independent journalist covering a troubling field.

Lots of people – mainly men – have told me how much they'd love to have my job. I just don't happen to be one of them. Not anymore.

35

Dead Last

We live in a world of winners. It's a world where the also-rans are ignored, and those who finish at the back of the pack may as well have never entered the race at all.

So, what about residents of that world who *never* win; or, nearly always, don't even finish? What sort of mantel do *they* use to exhibit their non-awards?

For that matter, if you never got an award or accolade for anything, was your life therefore meaningless?

When one of my auto history books was being prepared for publication, the editor sent me a copy of the blurb that would be used to advertise it in the publisher's catalog. Among other plaudits intended to stimulate sales, I was referred to as an "award-winning" author.

How sheepish, how inconsequential, I felt when informing the editor that I'd never won an award for anything. Ever. He'd assumed that every author worthy of publication must have at least a few badges of honor to show for his or her efforts.

Largely because I've always lacked a competitive spirit, only rarely have I ever competed for anything. How could I? Those of us who are never winners would be fools to present ourselves for consideration. Losing is a foregone conclusion, for good reason. No matter what the competition is about, in our eyes there is *always* someone better, somebody more talented or skilled; and yes, someone way more competent.

The winners among us seldom, if ever, understand what life is like for those who are invariably rejected, turned down, removed from competition, or ignored. Or, all of the above.

Not only winners, but the in-betweeners who sometimes

succeed and sometimes not, typically fail to grasp the concept of a person who runs dead last at virtually everything. It may even appear threatening in some weird way. In their narrow universe, everybody runs a good race, winding up at least in the middle of the pack. Nobody finishes last every time. How is that possible?

Having been a mail carrier for a while in my late teens, I was accustomed to walking substantial distances – often hauling a heavy mailbag. Several friends had become active in race walking, and I thought I'd give it a try. Perhaps walking could be the lone athletic endeavor in which I could compete, however modestly.

In my single walking race – six mile-long laps around a large city park – I came in fifth out of six entrants. The fellow I "beat" was an authentic amateur athlete: a bicycle racer. For me, that was a record day. And I still have the genuine plastic trophy given to finishers, to prove my prowess. It's packed away somewhere at present; but if I ever find it again, that cheap plastic award is going on display, as a reminder that once in my life, at least, I came in *second* to last.

For the "dead last" among us, there's little point competing in anything, because you know the result already. You knew it long ago, the first time you tried to compete. If ten people are participating, who will be tenth? We will. Always. No exceptions.

It's one of the few certainties in life, for the *compleat* incompetent.

36

Incompetence vs. Failure

Life isn't fair. President Jimmy Carter made that comment during his ill-fated Administration, and was castigated for it. However, he was indisputably correct.

We all know there are plenty of people in the world who lack competence, yet manage to succeed famously. Some, in fact, have led notoriously incompetent worklives, while attaining levels of success – including fame and fortune – that ordinary folks could barely dream about.

Conversely, who can say how many highly competent people never reach even the *bottom* step on that fantasy ladder of success, much less enjoy a steady climb upward? We can be stymied in our progress through life by personal problems, by making unwise choices, by tying ourselves to the wrong people – and of course, by pure chance.

We seldom hear about the *un*successful. History, like life, is written about (and by) the achievers. How many times do we read or hear about John Smith, "a successful (list occupation here)." Fred Furd, who never made it, doesn't even get the dignity of being called unsuccessful. He's just ignored.

You may have written the Great American Novel, but if you can't find anyone who will pay attention to it, much less publish your words, it may as well have not been written. You might possess great skill as a performer or an athlete; but for a multitude of reasons, no agent or scout ever seems to notice your presence or your prowess. Your ideas on economics, on the political scene, on technology or anything else, might provide a valuable solution to real-world problems; but they're words written on a feeble wind if you can't induce someone of consequence to pay attention to them.

Incompetence vs. Failure

Simply put, competence and success do not necessarily go hand in hand. Neither do incompetence and failure. Still, the two are intertwined, and one does at least *tend* to lead to the other. Exhibiting a lack of ability in everything one tries isn't much of a recipe for potential success, after all.

At the same time, highly competent people do have a lot more opportunities open up to them in the course of their lives. Statistically speaking, there's a stronger chance that at least one of them might be likely to lead that fortunate individual onto a secure pathway toward success.

Plenty of other factors enter the picture: determination, persistence, canniness, cleverness, and yes, perhaps the ability to deceive. It's certainly not uncommon for people who realize they're below average in capability to search for – and often find – ways to circumvent that inconvenient lack in their personal makeup. Some of the most ardent status-seekers, for example, spend much of their time trying to discern weakness in their competitors or opponents, then come up with methods to make that person look bad and themselves appear good.

The irony, for myself and for many other failures, is that we didn't expect, or ask for, all that much. In my case, getting just one piece of some value published by a significant publication. That single success would have moved me out of the utterly-worthless league.

Wealth? Not needed. Fame? Secondary, at best. Admiration? Never thought such a thing was possible.

No, just one tiny swatch of success, in the form of a single article, book, essay, op-ed, anything, of which I could be proud: some evidence of having contributed a teeny sliver of value to the world. About the closest I've come, in all these years, has been writing a biography of Robert Fulton for young readers. And possibly, turning out hundreds of thousands of hopefully-helpful words for consumers about buying used cars.

Instead, I spent my "literary" career mainly writing about a subject I'd once enjoyed, but grew to detest. By doing so, I was encouraging (at least indirectly) people to drive, which meant wasting gasoline, polluting the environment, and devoting their rapt attention to a machine that's ultimately of no consequence at all: the automobile.

Then again, maybe the optimists, those who see the bright side, are right. Perhaps it really is more important to lead an honest, forthright, scandal-free life, devoid of greed, avarice and other wickedness, than it is to rack up evidence of worldly success. Maybe so. Still, wouldn't it be nice if the non-winners among us finally got a little taste of the recognition that others see as their due, every day. Just one time. Wouldn't that be lovely.

37

So, aren't we all good at something?

For the all-around incompetent, there are no limits to our lack of capability. Even *sleeping* falls into my catalog of incompetence, as I've been an insomniac nearly all my life. Think you've had trouble with jet lag? My two recent long-term stays in Paris, to work on book projects, turned into sleep-free ordeals that lasted not for hours, or days, but for weeks. Two weeks after arrival the last time, I'd still not slept one minute during the night. The only time I could get a couple of hours' worth was in the afternoon. Not the best schedule to maintain in the fabled City of Lights.

Yet even I, if you've had the fortitude to read this far, have experienced an occasional mild success that could conceivably be called a reflection of competence.

As stated early on, one of my two authentic skills, dating from childhood, was spelling. And the opportunity I once had to display that skill before a sizable audience turned into something of a disaster, a personal loss that I never quite got over.

It was an example of the fact that, even when lifelong incompetents such as myself manage to do something well for a change, reality steps in. Immediately, it delivers a staggering blow to remind us that we don't really belong in the realm of the successful.

At Chicago's James G. Blaine elementary school, I'd thought I was the best speller in the city, maybe in the country. I felt a bit like Paul Newman in his 1962 film *The Hustler*, where he knew – absolutely knew for sure – that he was the best pool player in the world. As his paramour, played by Piper Laurie, put it, most men *never* get such a feeling in their entire lives, about anything.

Incompetent

After handily winning our school Spelling Bee, I proceeded a few weeks later to the District contest. Again, I vanquished all contenders soundly, spending a relatively leisurely afternoon onstage.

Then came the City of Chicago competition. Here, reality finally displayed its ugly head, turning what might have been a tale of triumph into a horror story. Spelling Bees were different in 1951. Today, contestants not only arrive at the contest well prepared, they're given lists containing the actual words that will be used in the competition. Unbelievable! In my eyes, that's tantamount to cheating.

I had no preparation whatsover. All my spelling ability was contained within my brain, and it wouldn't have occurred to me – or to anyone – to try and prepare in any way. All I had to do was show up. And therein, as Shakespeare put it, lay "the rub."

The Spelling Bee was to take place at the Civic Opera House, at the edge of Chicago's downtown Loop. We lived about 6 miles to the north. The plan was for my father to drive me to the evening event, doubtless like the fathers of virtually all the other contestants.

Except that mine was drunk. Sitting in some tavern somewhere, on the night when his eldest son had, for once in a lifetime, a chance to shine. His failure to come home at dinnertime was nothing new. After work, he nearly always stopped at a bar for an hour, two, or more. This night was no exception.

Because my younger brother was barely more than a toddler, my mother couldn't leave him to accompany me to the Bee. Thankfully, the man living in the apartment above us – father of my short-term girlfriend at age 10 – stepped in, taking me to the TV studio inside the Civic Opera House in his new Plymouth.

After locating a babysitter, my mother took the elevated train downtown later in the evening. I didn't see her until after the Spelling Bee was over, and we stopped at a restaurant where I downed a big ice cream sundae to try and settle my tormented stomach. Tasty it was, but the remedy didn't work.

I lost. Came in fourth, ironically beaten by two of the kids I had vanquished so handily in the District competition. The winning girl

So, aren't we all good at **something?**

got a trip to Washington D.C. to compete in the national event. Second and third place winners took home a set of encyclopedias. Me? I got the same pen and pencil set given to each contestant.

When it was announced that my spelling of the word "regatta" was incorrect, I was stunned. Never before had I missed a word. And this seemed like such an easy one.

Not that I'd ever heard it before. Working-class Chicagoans didn't go to regattas. If they owned boats of any kind, they were rowboats, used to go fishing on Lake Michigan or up in Wisconsin. Certainly not the kind of high-falluting sailing ships that competed in regattas.

Whether I hadn't heard the word correctly, or was just confused by that time, I'll never know. I spelled by means of sounding out words, and should have been able to deduce this one without difficulty. But I didn't. I was Number Four, not Number One.

Naturally, I was the only contestant to arrive alone, unaccompanied, unsupported. Did that affect the outcome? Probably not. After I was eliminated, the words got a lot tougher. No telling whether I'd have been able to rely on sounding-out and maintain my record of unbroken success.

As gamblers often bemoan when they've had a bad session at the track or the tables, it just wasn't my day.

38

Conclusion

"Don't mistake activity with achievement."
– Late basketball player/coach John Wooden

"If you can do a half-assed job of anything, you're a one-eyed man in a kingdom of the blind."
– Late author Kurt Vonnegut

History, we've observed, is written by – and about – the successful. Almost inevitably, those who fall into that category fail to notice, much less take any note of, the failures of the world. Competent folks' achievements are the ones that are recounted and recorded for posterity. The rest of us are basically invisible, unseen, unconsidered.

How often do we read about so-and-so, who's had a "successful" career as a whatever. In contrast, how often are we informed of anyone who qualifies as a "failed" member of that occupation or profession? Or of life in general.

Oh, occasionally, a few words are stated about someone who never found a suitable path through life. But not so much is ever said about anyone who's actually failed, whether through incompetence or for any other reason. Not unless it's meant as an object lesson, warning younger folks to take steps to avoid such an ignominious fate themselves.

Among the lies we live by, insistence that hard work inevitably leads to success is the biggest – and the most devastating. It falls right behind "there's a job for everybody who wants one," and "persistence pays." Such assertions are practically guaranteed to make the recipient feel his lack of success is his own fault. Therefore, he must be worthless.

Many of us cannot help but wonder why we turned out so short on capabilities, while others wound up with far more than their fair share. Was I born at the wrong time, in the wrong place? Probably. Of course, millions of other strivers might also have been happier (as well as successful) if their circumstances, upbringing, and career paths — whether freely chosen or forced upon them — had been markedly different.

Mainly, though, like so much else in life, it's a question of luck and chance, as well as competence. Some of us find the way; others don't. Admittedly, many of us undertake a string of poor life choices, stemming from our lack of ability and consequent self-confidence. So it goes.

Rightly or wrongly, we incompetents, we underachievers, seem to wind up stuck on the sidelines of life. If this book has any purpose, other than providing some tidbits of terminal incompetence by someone who's truly been there, it's to affirm our affinity with all the other less-than-competent people out there. If you're one of us, remember that you're not alone. We're a minority, true, but a more sizable one than might be expected — albeit largely unknown. After all, who — except for the aging author of these words — would be so foolish as to admit to a frightful level of incompetence? It's not something most of us ever talk about, or acknowledge.

How much does competence really matter, anyway? Is achievement all that important to a meaningful life?

Even the least competent among us *could* have done better. A *little* better. We could have accepted that our present path was never going to lead anywhere, and simply abandoned it, seeking another that might have led to a more promising result.

In my youth, due to gullibility and shamefully frequent intoxication, I was easily swayed by others into acts that were dreadful and destructive. I also held views that were less than generous and honest.

Incompetent

Once I stopped drinking at age 30, I settled into a life that I hoped would stand in stark contrast, striving in the direction of ethics, honesty, integrity, and generosity. Though I've not necessarily been as kind or cordial as I would have liked, I am not displeased by my progress in other areas. A case can be made, of course, that virtues such as these are more important in evaluating the worthiness of one's life than tangible successes, recognition, wealth, fame – the familiar standards we've learned to overvalue in our celebrity-focused culture.

Excessively high expectations play a role, too. When feeling that I've accomplished especially little, I'm often reminded of a physician I once read about. Despite a hugely accomplished life as a doctor, augmented by achievements in a host of other areas, he committed suicide at an early age. Why? Despite having achieved twenty times what a normal person might have, he felt he'd done nothing worthwhile with his life.

Despite all that's been said in these pages, in the end I'm glad I didn't land a successful literary career at an early age. Why? Because, by struggling at the lower end of my particular occupation, I never lost sight of the trials and ordeals that so many of the unaccomplished go through, with little or no light at the end of anyone's tunnel. Better to have failed and understood this, than to be successful but oblivious.

So, fellow incompetents, if you haven't already, may you enjoy at least a *little* taste of success. But not so much that you forget about the rest of us, who keep plodding along and will never make it, despite our best efforts. That's reality.

About the Author

James M. Flammang has been a journalist, writer, and editor for his entire working life. Since the 1980s, he's covered the automobile business as an independent journalist. In addition to contributing product reviews and articles to such publications as autoMedia, Kelley Blue Book, CarsDirect, J.D. Power, cars.com, Consumer Guide, and the *Chicago Tribune*, Flammang has authored more than thirty books. Most of them were about automotive history, but he also has written six books for children. Flammang is a member of the Freelancers Union, International Motor Press Association, and Midwest Automotive Media Association (past president).

Lately, Flammang has been easing away from cars, to focus on books: mostly essays and memoirs, plus a bit of fiction, establishing TK Press to publish his work. *Mr. Maurice Knows It All....* was the first. Next was the *Tirekicking Used Car Buyer's Guide*, now followed by *Incompetent*. Coming soon: *Absurdities, Untied Knots, Work Hurts, Hotel Life,* and *Fraidy-Cat*. Born in Chicago, Flammang lives just outside that city with his wife, advisor and editor, Marianne.

www.ingramcontent.com/pod-product-compliance
Lightning Source LLC
Chambersburg PA
CBHW070614300426
44113CB00010B/1530